The Tay

pocket mountains ltd

Published by
Pocket Mountains Ltd
Holm Street, Moffat, DG10 9EB
www.pocketmountains.com

ISBN: 978-1-907025-433

Text and photography © Keith Fergus

Introduction

Rivers have been at the centre of Scottish life for thousands of years. For the earliest settlers a river meant survival – a source of food, drinking water and transport. Over the centuries, villages, towns and all of Scotland's cities have grown and developed along the banks of a river.

From the Industrial Revolution, when Scotland was one of the manufacturing powerhouses of Europe, until the long decline of heavy industry in the 20th century, rivers were integral to Scotland's economic development.

As towns and cities attempt to reinvent themselves in the wake of that decline, rivers and riverbanks are crucial to regeneration, providing key destinations for residential developments, offices, leisure and recreation. Water activities such as rowing, sailing, kayaking, canyoning and fishing are increasingly popular, and wildlife is making a comeback as the environment begins to recover from pollution.

From source to sea, a river passes through a variety of landscapes – from mountains to hills, towns to cities, countryside to concrete – and the best way to discover the scenery, wildlife, architecture and history is to walk.

The increasing number of paths and walkways along riverbanks present plenty of opportunities to explore. Whatever your ability – walking at high or low level, tackling tough terrain or a simple route – this series offers something for everyone.

The River Tay

The Tay may be unique amongst Scotland's major rivers in that its source lies many miles from where the river's course actually begins. Its source is generally considered to be a small lochan at the head of Allt Coire Laoigh high on the slopes of Ben Lui, near Tyndrum. The burn flows into the Rivers Cononish and Dochart before finally, nearly 19 miles later, reaching Loch Tay. But even then the River Tay only makes its first appearance when it spills from the eastern end of this 15-mile-long loch at Kenmore.

From here, the Tay charts a sinuous course through some of the finest scenery in Perthshire, before becoming tidal at Perth. However, it is still another 20 miles before the Tay finally reaches the sea just beyond Dundee, its mouth bounded by Buddon Ness in Angus and Fife's Tentsmuir Point. This 120-mile journey makes Scotland's longest river.

The Tay is an immense river in every respect. As well as being notable for its length, it carries the largest volume of water of any river in the UK, with a vast catchment of more than 5000 square km – including sizeable tributaries such as the Ericht, Tummel, Garry and Lyon. By the time it reaches the Firth of Tay, it carries more water than the Thames and

River Tay from Birnam Hill

Severn combined and extends to a width of almost three miles. Several dams and lochs, including Loch Rannoch, Loch Tummel and Loch Tay, help control water levels, particularly during heavy spates.

On its journey, the River Tay flows through a wide-ranging landscape – initially characterised by wild mountains and steep-sided glens, but with a distinct softening as it crosses the Highland Boundary Fault at Dunkeld. From here, the Tay meanders through some of the most fertile farmland in Scotland before reaching the coast.

Not surprisingly, the walking to be had around the Tay is also delightfully varied, from big mountain climbs to simple countryside rambles and scenic coastal strolls. Away from the bulk of mountains like Ben Lawers and Schiehallion, lower summits such as Birnam Hill, Kinnoull Hill and the Sidlaws offer fine walking with views over the river and beyond.

Several routes in this guide start from or near attractive and historic towns and villages, such as Kenmore, Aberfeldy and Dunkeld, each of these edged by wildlife-rich woodland. The Tay's two cities, Perth and Dundee, also boast a fascinating cultural history, while bracing coastal walks can be enjoyed along the Firth of Tay at Broughty Ferry, Newburgh and Tentsmuir Point.

The routes in this guide have been chosen to illustrate the diversity of walking to be found on and near the banks of the River Tay as it travels from source to sea. Many of these routes are circular to take in the best of the scenery in the area that surrounds each stage of the river's journey. The walks also highlight the wildlife, architecture and history to be found along the way.

Luminaries such as Robert Burns, William Wordsworth and J M W Turner wrote of or painted the Tay in its many forms, each encouraging tourists of the day to discover it for themselves. Today, tourism remains hugely important for much of Highland Perthshire, although the Tay and surrounding tributaries now play host to rather more active pursuits, including white water rafting, canyoning and kayaking.

River tales

It was during the 1st century AD that the River Tay was recorded by the Roman historian Tacitus as *Taus*, while a later Roman name for it was possibly *Tamia*. However, its present-day derivation of 'strong', 'silent' or 'flowing' seems to stem from the Brythonic word *Tausa*. Another of Scotland's great rivers, The Tweed, also has Brythonic origins, its name translating from *Tau*.

Like the River Tweed, the Tay is one of Scotland's premier salmon rivers. The UK's largest rod-caught salmon was landed near Dunkeld in 1922 when Georgina Ballantine reeled in a 64lb fish.

A significant salmon industry built up

around the River Tay some 500 years ago as the fish became a valuable item of trade, while stake nets were established along the Tay Estuary in the late 1700s. Stepping further back in time, a Pictish carving of a salmon was discovered near the River Isla, another of the Tay's main tributaries. Salmon may also have been part of the Mesolithic hunter-gatherer diet when the area around Tentsmuir Point was settled 10,000 years ago.

More is known about settlement in the area during the Iron Age, the history of which can be explored at the Scottish Crannog Centre on the banks of Loch Tay near Kenmore. Elsewhere, around 1500 years ago, the Picts built several hill forts along the Tay, the best example of which adorns the summit of Moncreiffe Hill on the outskirts of Perth.

In 83AD, as the Romans slowly edged their way north through Scotland, they paused at the confluence of the River Tay and River Almond and established a fort called Bertha, the precursor to Perth (which would subsequently develop just downriver). The Romans also headed east and utilised the panoramic vantage point of Dundee Law.

Near to Perth, at the old Pictish capital of Scone, Kenneth MacAlpin, King of Scots, arrived in 843AD to establish a nation and a Royal Seat. At the time, Perth vied with Dunfermline to be considered Scotland's capital.

For Perth, the river has been both a blessing and a curse. It is here that the Tay reaches its highest navigable point, with boats plying the river between Perth and the Outer Firth since medieval times. For a time, shipbuilding was a prominent industry, with timber floated along the river to several small shipyards at Perth, while the town was also once a busy trading port with goods such as wool, salt, coal and salmon exported to Northern Europe and the Baltics.

But with Perth occupying such a low-lying site, the Tay has also brought its fair share of misery. Major flooding has been recorded as far back as 1210 – when the one bridge across the river was destroyed – as well as more recent events in 1990 and 1993 when parts of the city were inundated. The highest ever recorded flood took place here in 1814, when the river rose to 7m above its normal level. Today, the city is protected by a system of major flood defences.

The Tay also helped Dundee develop internationally as a sizeable port and, for 150 years or so, as a premier whaling port. Hundreds of ships were built here, including the *RRS Discovery* – now moored by the banks of the Tay at Discovery Point.

A thriving textile industry, primarily the production of linen for sailcloth, was a major employer, but it was the city's 'three Js' – jute, jam and journalism – that really drove the Dundee economy during the 19th century. The production of jute for sacks, in particular, was vital to its development, at one time employing more than 35,000 workers (around one-third of the city's population).

The jute mills are long gone, but engineering, telecommunications, publishing, digital media and computer programming have given Dundee a new lease of life in recent years.

How to use this guide

The 25 walks in this guidebook run geographically from the source of the Tay on the slopes of Ben Lui to the Firth of Tay, where it empties into the sea just beyond Dundee. Wherever possible, the start/finish for each walk is easily accessible by public transport and, if not, there is car parking nearby. The majority of the walks are easily reached from villages and towns along the length of the River Tay, with access to shops, places to eat, accommodation and public toilets.

Each route begins with an introduction detailing the terrain walked, the start/finish point (and grid reference), the distance covered, the average time to walk the route and the relevant Ordnance Survey (OS) map.

Public transport information is also detailed, although this may change from time to time and should be checked before commencing any of the walks in this guide (travelinescotland.com).

A sketch map shows the main topographical details of the area and the route. The map is intended only to give the reader an idea of the terrain, and should not be followed for navigation – the relevant OS map should be used for this purpose.

Every route has an estimated round-trip time. This is for rough guidance only and should help in planning, especially when daylight hours are limited. In winter, or after heavy rain, extra time should be added to allow for difficult conditions underfoot.

Risks and how to avoid them

Some of the routes in this guidebook are challenging hillwalks while others cover more remote terrain. The weather in Scotland can change suddenly, reducing visibility to only a few yards. Winter walking brings distinct challenges, particularly the limited daylight hours and the temperature – over higher ground, temperatures can fall well below freezing. Please take this into consideration before commencing any of the hillwalks in this guide. Preparation should begin well before you set out, and your choice of route should reflect your fitness, the conditions underfoot and the regional weather forecasts.

None of the hillwalks in this guide should be attempted without the relevant OS map or equivalent at 1:50,000 (or 1:25,000) and a compass.

Even in summer, warm waterproof clothing is advisable, and footwear that is comfortable and supportive with good grips is a must. Don't underestimate how much food and water you need and remember to take any medication required, including reserves in case of illness or delay. Do not rely on receiving a mobile phone signal when out walking, particularly away from built-up areas. It is a good idea to leave a route description with a friend or relative in case of emergency.

There is a route for almost all levels of fitness in this guide, but it is important to know your limitations. Even for an experienced walker, colds, aches and pains can turn an easy walk into an ordeal.

Those routes that venture into the hills or rough terrain assume some knowledge of navigation with use of map and compass, though these skills are not difficult to learn. Use of Global Positioning System (GPS) is becoming more common; however, while GPS can help pinpoint your location on the map in zero visibility, it cannot tell you where to go next and, like a mobile phone, should not be relied upon.

Only a few walks in this guide cross hill or mountain terrain and in winter it is recommended that you take an ice axe and crampons – and know how to use them – on these. Such skills will improve confidence and the ease with which such a route can be completed. They will also help you to avoid or escape potentially dangerous areas if you lose your way. The Mountaineering Council of Scotland provides training and information (mcofs.org.uk). However, for most of the routes in this guide, proficiency in walking and navigation is sufficient.

Access

Until the Land Reform (Scotland) Act was introduced in 2003, the 'right to roam' in Scotland was a result of continued negotiation between government bodies, interest groups and landowners. In many respects, the Act simply reinforces the strong tradition of public access to the countryside of Scotland for recreational purposes. However, a key difference is that under the Act the right of access depends on whether it is exercised responsibly.

Landowners also have an obligation not to unreasonably prevent or deter those seeking access. The responsibilities of the public and land managers are set out in the Scottish Outdoor Access Code (outdooraccess-scotland.com).

The walks in this guidebook cross land that is only fully accessible due to the co-operation of landowners, local councils and residents. Some of the routes pass through farms, golf courses and streets, and near homes and gardens.

Cyclists and horse riders often use the paths and tracks, and anglers and canoeists may use the river and riverbanks. Consideration for others should be taken into account at all times and the Scottish Outdoor Access Code must be followed.

At certain times of the year special restrictions are implemented at low level and on the hills, and these should be respected. These often concern farming, shooting and forest activities: if you are in any doubt, ask. Signs are usually posted at popular access points with details: there should be no presumption of a right of access to all places at all times.

The right of access does not extend to the use of motor vehicles on private or estate roads.

Seasonal Restrictions

Red and Sika Deer Stalking:
Stags: 1 July to 20 October
Hinds: 21 October to 15 February
Deer may also be culled at other times for welfare reasons. The seasons for Fallow and Roe deer (less common) are also longer. Many estates provide advance notice of shoots on their websites.

Grouse Shooting:
12 August to 10 December

Forestry:
Felling: All Year
Planting: November to May

Heather Burning:
September to April

Lambing:
March to May – although dogs should be kept on leads at all times near livestock.

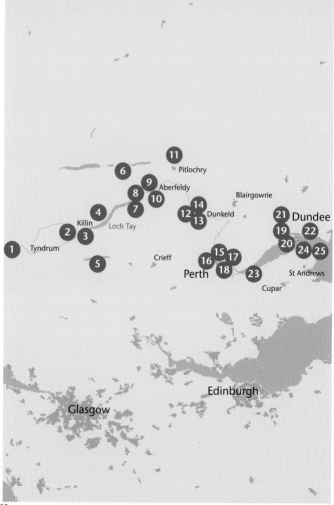

Tyndrum
Killin
Loch Tay
Aberfeldy
Pitlochry
Blairgowrie
Dunkeld
Dundee
Crieff
Perth
St Andrews
Cupar
Glasgow
Edinburgh

The Walks

Ben Lui and Allt Coire Laoigh

Ben Lui

Ben Lui and Beinn a' Chleibh

Distance 19.5km/12 miles
Time 7 hours
Start/Finish Tyndrum GR NN330304
Terrain Glen and mountain paths, sections of pathless terrain. Some steep ascents and descents
Map OS Landranger 50
Public transport Regular Scotrail Service from Glasgow and Mallaig to Tyndrum (Upper Station) and from Glasgow and Oban to Tyndrum (Lower Station). Regular Scottish Citylink Service 914 from Glasgow and Fort William to Tyndrum

Ben Lui is often regarded as one of the finest mountains in the Southern Highlands, a complex peak with great ridges and a renowned corrie – and on its slopes lies the source of the River Tay. Tackled with neighbouring Beinn a' Chleibh, this is a challenging route, but if you dislike exposure or the weather is against you, the section to Coire Gaothach is a great walk in its own right and well within the reach of most walkers.

▶ At Tyndrum, join Lower Station Road and walk past cottages and a campsite until the road sweeps round to Tyndrum Lower Station. Cross the railway line with care at a level crossing and go straight on along a broad track, signposted for Cononish and Ben Lui, climbing gradually into conifer woodland.

▶ After around 2km, the path exits the woodland via a gate to meet a track which runs beside the clear waters of the River Cononish. Turn right here and bear west through the Ben Lui National Nature Reserve – livestock graze here so keep dogs on leads.

▶ It's a long walk in to mighty Ben Lui, but this allows you to appreciate this natural amphitheatre, with the steep slopes of Beinn Dubhchraig to the south and the shapely profile of Beinn Chuirn and the spectacular waterfall of Eas Anie up ahead. At the head of the glen, dominating everything around it, is Ben Lui itself.

▶ Once at the farm at Cononish, go straight on at a crossroads, pass through a gate and proceed along the track. With the bulky profile of Ben Oss to the south, the landscape becomes wilder. Ahead rise the seemingly impenetrable slopes of Ben Lui but, as you approach, it is possible to pick out a line of ascent. There is also a great view along the Allt Coire Laoigh, which is generally recognised as the source of the River Tay.

▶ Drop down to the waters of the Allt an Rund, where the track comes to an abrupt end. A couple of rocky steps make for a reasonably simple crossing, although be prepared for the possibility of wet feet. Once across, a clear path climbs steeply past the ruin of an old cottage and to the right of the pretty Allt Coire Ghaothaich. In season, the path is lined with wildflowers, while rowan trees cling improbably to the riverbank.

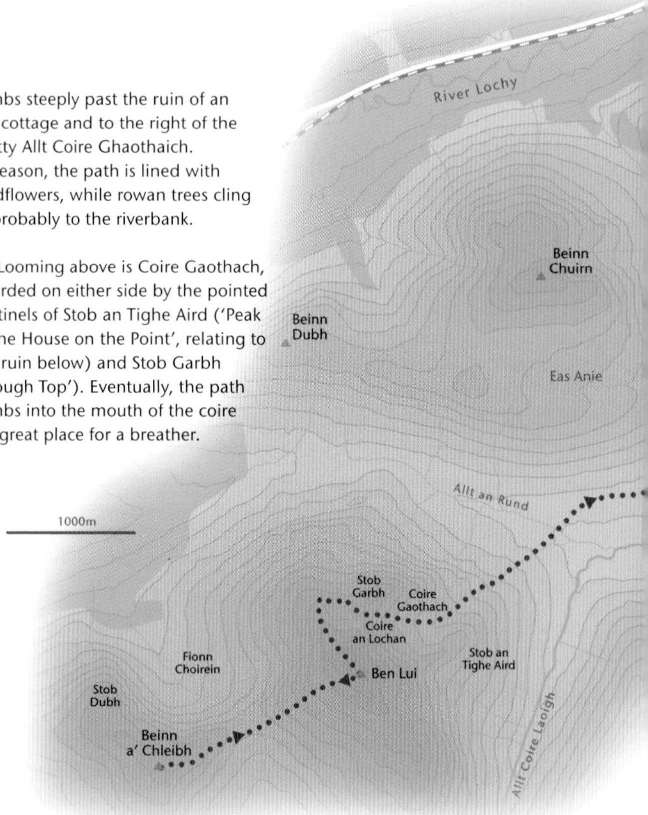

► Looming above is Coire Gaothach, guarded on either side by the pointed sentinels of Stob an Tighe Aird ('Peak of the House on the Point', relating to the ruin below) and Stob Garbh ('Rough Top'). Eventually, the path climbs into the mouth of the coire – a great place for a breather.

River Lochy

Beinn
Chuirn

Beinn
Dubh

Eas Anie

Allt an Rund

1000m

Stob
Garbh

Coire
Gaothach

Coire
an Lochan

Fionn
Choirein

Stob an
Tighe Aird

Stob
Dubh

Ben Lui

Allt Coire Laoigh

Beinn
a' Chleibh

Gold Rush Although now geared towards passing travellers, the village of Tyndrum is perhaps best known for an association with mining that dates back some 600 years when the surrounding hills supplied King James I with silver. Lead was also mined here commercially from the 18th century but, in more recent times, attention has returned to a much bigger prize: gold. An Australian company has gained approval to reopen an old gold mine at Cononish, though production has yet to begin.

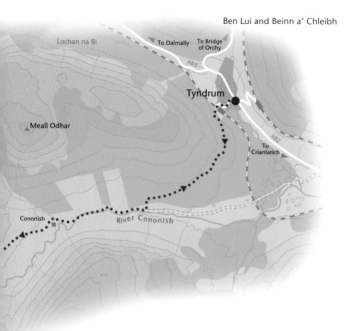

► It's now decision time. The path continues through Coire Gaothach to climb the steep cliffs that lead directly to the summit of Ben Lui – however, it is exposed. For many, a better route is via Ben Lui's northeast ridge. With the pronounced nose of Stob Garbh above, bear right from the path and cross grassy ground into Coire an Lochain, passing to the right of a lochan before climbing west up steep slopes and onto the airy ridge of Stob Garbh. From here, head left and follow a path south across rough, rocky ground to gain Ben Lui's 1130m summit.

► The tricky navigation is done for now with a path descending easily, albeit steeply, southwest from Ben Lui. It is then a stiff, zigzag pull onto Beinn a' Chleibh which, at 916m, just reaches Munro status. It gives a fine view back to Ben Lui, as well as west to Ben Cruachan – the highest point in Argyll and Bute.

► From here, retrace your steps to Ben Lui. Real care must be taken when descending Stob Garbh into Coire Gaothach and down to Allt an Rund. Once back on the track, it is a simple return journey to Tyndrum.

River Cononish from Ben Lui

Ben Lawers from Sron a' Chlachain

Sron a' Chlachain and Creag Bhuidhe

Distance 3.5km/2.25 miles
Time 1 hour 45
Start/Finish Breadalbane Park,
Killin GR NN573331
Terrain Parkland and hill paths.
Some steep ascents and descents
Map OS Landranger 51
Public transport Regular Kingshouse
Travel Service C60 between
Callander and Killin

Although relatively short, any thoughts that this walk from Killin is a simple stroll to a nearby viewpoint are quickly banished. Several steep sections by way of Sron a' Chlachain must be negotiated before you gain the summit of Creag Bhuidhe. Once there, however, the views over Loch Tay and beyond are magnificent. The route crosses open countryside, so keep dogs under close control.

▶ Starting from Killin village centre, enter Breadalbane Park from Main Street (just north of the school). Take the left-hand path, which skirts the edge of the park, and continue past several houses to a fork just before a gate. The left fork leads to nearby Fingal's Stone – said to be the burial place of Celtic giant and warrior Fingal who died at the hands of a rival at Eilean Lubhair on Loch Dochart. Legend has it that Fingal's body was subsequently found at the Falls of Dochart at the southern edge of Killin.

▶ Take the right fork to climb west along a grassy path over a field to a stile. Beyond this, the path rises steeply through oak woodland before swinging left and out onto open hillside. Once above the treeline, the gradient steepens again to reach the first viewpoint. This is a good spot for a breather, with a fine outlook east along the length of Loch Tay.

▶ Continue to a fork and branch right. Although this makes for a slightly easier ascent than the left option, it is still a

Standing Guard Sron a' Chlachain, which translates from Gaelic as 'Nose-shaped Hill of the Village', looms over Killin, close to the banks of Loch Tay. It is here, at the head of the loch, that two of its main feeder rivers, the Dochart and the Lochay, converge – an impressive sight when seen from the high hillside. The views elsewhere are just as rewarding, sweeping from nearby Beinn Ghlas and Ben Lawers to Ben Vorlich in the south and the deep defile of Glen Lochay and much of the old county of Breadalbane to the west.

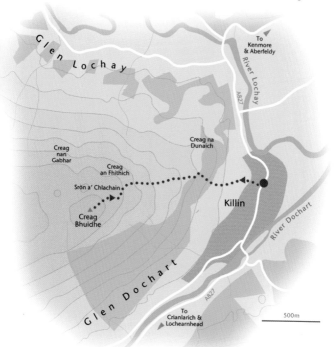

stiff pull and the path is not always distinct as it cuts between the steep crags. It soon reaches a crest, however, rejoining the left-hand path with great views over the rough ridge of Meall nan Tarmachan and the sprawling Ben Lawers massif.

▶ From the crest, head right and follow another steep path which is thankfully a lot easier than it looks as it zigzags

through a breach in the craggy rock face. A gradual climb over open hillside then leads to one final steep pull, the path running to the right of an old wall and passing a small cairn to reach the large cairn that marks the summit of Creag Bhuidhe.

▶ The only feasible means of return is to retrace your steps, enjoying the views all the way back to Killin.

Loch Tay from Sron a' Chlachain

River Lochay

The Falls of Dochart

The Falls of Dochart and Loch Tay

Distance 5km/3 miles
Time 1 hour 30
Start/Finish Falls of Dochart, Killin GR NN572324
Terrain Pavement, countryside, lochside and riverbank paths
Map OS Landranger 51
Public transport Regular Kingshouse Travel Service C60 between Callander and Killin

The tumbling Falls of Dochart at the southern edge of Killin make a wonderfully picturesque start point for this walk. Using a network of easy paths, this route meanders downstream to explore the place where the Rivers Dochart and Lochay converge at the head of Loch Tay.

► Begin from the A827 on the south bank of the River Dochart, beside the Falls of Dochart – a spectacular sight when the river is in spate. Cross the bridge over the Dochart and follow the road as it swings right and through the village of Killin, the rugged Meall nan Tarmachan and Ben Lawers towering above.

► Once beyond the police station, bear right onto Lyon Road and pass the little corrugated iron St Fillan's Episcopal Church. Turn right beside a small car park and head through a gate to the right of some public toilets. From here, turn left onto a path which was once part of the branchline of the Callander to Oban Railway. This section opened in 1886 and ran to a pier on Loch Tay, where passengers could join the steamer service which plied the length of the loch.

► Follow this wooded path across the River Lochay, with tantalising glimpses of Loch Tay, as well as Creag an Fhithich and other rounded hills that rise above its southern shores, along the way.

Pull up a Pew Constructed from standardised corrugated iron sheets on a wooden frame, churches such as St Fillan's in Killin were common during Victorian times, when they were known as tin tabernacles. St Fillan's Episcopal Church was built in 1876 by the 7th Marquis of Breadalbane as a place for his shooting parties to worship, and was known locally as the Grouse Chapel. Nearby is the distinctive white-harled Killin and Ardeonaig Parish Church, built in 1744. At its front is a memorial to the Reverend James Stewart, one-time minister of Killin who first translated the New Testament into Scots Gaelic, published in 1767.

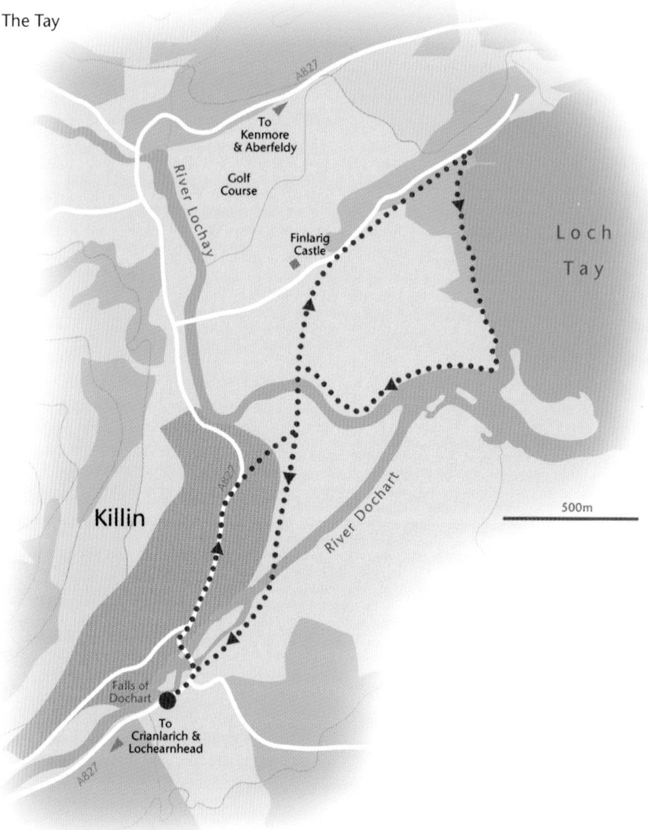

A827

To
Kenmore
& Aberfeldy

River Lochay

Golf
Course

Finlarig
Castle

Loch
Tay

A827

Killin

River Dochart

500m

Falls of
Dochart

To
Crianlarich &
Lochearnhead

A827

► After around 1.25km, you come to the head of Loch Tay. Turn right here and follow a path along the sandy shore of the loch, skirting some oak woodland and passing a beach, a good spot to pause and soak up the views. Continue southwards, with the grassy path soon reaching the outflow of the Rivers Lochay and Dochart. Here, you can best appreciate the steep, rounded slopes of Sron a' Chlachain above Killin, with the outlook extending beyond to the Southern Highland giants of Ben More and Stob Binnein.

▶ Veer right here through a gate and continue along the north bank of the River Lochay, crossing sections of boardwalk. Go through a gate to skirt along the edge of a field, leaving it by another gate and turning left to return to the railway path.

▶ Cross the bridge over the River Lochay and begin to follow the path back towards Killin. However, instead of retracing your steps through the gate at the public toilets, continue straight on along the old railway line until the path turns right to meet Lyon Road. Go left here and, once past the Old Mart, turn left again onto a track that soon crosses a bridge over the Dochart.and follows the river upstream to reach a junction.

▶ Turn right here and head along a narrow road that runs parallel with the river, its fast-flowing waters now cutting through a heavily-wooded gorge. Continue past a couple of houses and back to the Falls of Dochart.

Island Burial The Falls of Dochart pass beneath the old stone Bridge of Dochart which dates back to 1760, although the central arch was rebuilt in 1831 following flood damage. It's a perfect vantage point for enjoying the falls, plus an island (Innis Bhuidhe) just downstream that is home to the Clan MacNab burial ground. An enclosure within the burial ground contains 15 graves, nine of which are the final resting places of clan chiefs. Although thought to have been in use since the 1700s, the island also holds a medieval grave slab that suggests earlier burials may have taken place here.

Meall Corranaich from Beinn Ghlas

Beinn Ghlas and Ben Lawers

Distance 10km/6.25 miles
Time 5 hours
Start/Finish Ben Lawers National
Nature Reserve Car Park
GR NN608379
Terrain Hill and mountain paths.
Some steep ascents and descents
Map OS Landranger 51
Public transport None to start

At 1214m (just short of 4000ft),
Ben Lawers is the highest point on
the range of hills that dominates
the skyline above Loch Tay. Nearby
Beinn Ghlas (1103m) – used here as
a stepping stone to reach the
summit of its more celebrated
neighbour – is also well into Munro
territory. With the start point
already at an altitude of 450m,
exploring these lofty peaks is not
quite as arduous as it sounds.

▶ Ben Lawers is one of nine mountains
– including seven Munros – that sit
within the Ben Lawers National Nature
Reserve, cared for by the National Trust

for Scotland. As such, the paths used
throughout this walk are maintained
to a high standard.

▶ From the car park, take the path
leading back to the road. Cross over
and follow the path on the other side,
beginning the gradual ascent through
the nature reserve. Carry straight on
past a turn-off for the Edramucky Trail
on the right to follow the path signed
for Ben Lawers.

▶ At first, this rises gradually alongside
birch and rowan before bearing right
over a burn and then dropping down to
cross the Edramucky Burn. From here,
the trail climbs steadily northwards
alongside a deer fence, with fine views
of Meall Corranaich across the glen.

▶ In due course, swing right away from
the burn, but continue to follow the line
of the fence to a gate. Beyond this,
continue to a fork where you take the
right branch (the left option marks the
route of descent) and follow the

Arctic-alpine Rarities An unusual coming together of lime-rich rock, altitude and
climate ensures that Ben Lawers attracts almost as many botanists as Munro-
baggers. Of particular interest are the arctic-alpine species that have drawn
botanists to the cliffs and slopes of Ben Lawers since the 1770s when colourful plant
communities were first discovered here. In amongst the yellow saxifrage, alpine
lady's-mantle, moss campion and purple saxifrage – all important species in their
own right – are some real rarities, with alpine gentian and alpine forget-me-not
found in only one or two other places in Britain.

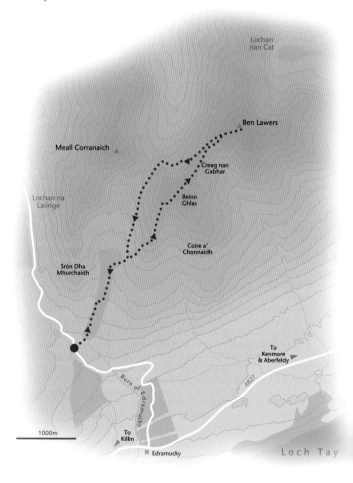

excellent path as it climbs more steeply up the lower slopes of Beinn Ghlas before zigzagging ever higher with great views opening out over Loch Tay. Once over a crest, the first sight of the undulating top of Beinn Ghlas rises ahead. There is some respite as the path levels out before a final steep, twisting ascent to the summit.

▶ With one summit gained and the top of Ben Lawers visible for the first time, attention now turns to the big one. Continue northeast, following the summit ridge as it narrows and drops to the bealach (pass) between Beinn Ghlas and Ben Lawers – with the latter's steep, folded crags directly ahead.

▶ Passing a path off to the left (remember this for the return route), the final push sees a steep climb up Ben Lawers' rocky slopes to a craggy, compact summit, adorned by a trig point and cairn. On a clear day, the views are extensive.

▶ For the return journey, first retrace your steps to the bealach but, instead of climbing back up Beinn Ghlas, bear right to join a good path that contours southwest around its northern flank, with wonderful views to Glen Lyon below. Here – and lower down near the car park – look for a scattering of shielings once used by shepherds as temporary shelters when grazing cattle on higher ground during the summer.

▶ Once across a burn, the path sweeps around the crags to reach the head of the glen, the grassy slopes of Meall Corranaich rising on the right. From here, the path descends gently until it reaches the outbound path at the base of Beinn Ghlas. Turn right onto this and retrace your steps to the car park.

....

On the Hoof It is thought that Ben Lawers (Beinn Labhair) translates from Gaelic as 'Mountain of the Hoof', with the name referring to the shape of the high peaks and deep corries of the wider Ben Lawers massif when seen from a distance. Another translation stems from *Labhair*, meaning 'loud' and pertaining to a nearby river or burn. Whatever the origins of its name, it's a formidable lump – and the highest peak in the Southern Highlands. On a clear day, the magnificent view from the summit includes the hills above Bridge of Orchy, the sharp cone of Schiehallion, the twin peaks of Ben Vorlich and Stuc a' Chroin – not to mention the length of Loch Tay.

Ben Lawers from Beinn Ghlas

Beinn Ghlas from Ben Lawers

Loch Earn from Ben Vorlich

Ben Vorlich and Ben Our

Distance **10km/6.25 miles**
Time **5 hours**
Start/Finish **East Gate, Ardvorlich House GR NN634233**
Terrain **Hill and mountain paths and tracks. Some sections of pathless and rough terrain**
Maps **OS Landranger 51 and 57**
Public transport **Regular Kingshouse Travel Service C60 from Callander and Killin to Lochearnhead, 5km from the start**

Rising high above Loch Earn, a few miles south of Loch Tay, Ben Vorlich is a landmark for those journeying alongside the Tay from Killin to Aberfeldy. Although steep in parts, the path to this vantage point over much of Stirlingshire and Perthshire is excellent. The neighbouring peak of Stuc a' Chroin is often tagged on to a walk over Ben Vorlich, with the descent chiefly back along the same route, but a far more interesting way off Ben Vorlich is to descend via Ben Our. Be warned, though: some of the route traverses pathless terrain while the final, short descent to the main trail crosses rough ground.

► Start from the east gate of Ardvorlich House (limited parking along the roadside) just east of a roadbridge

over the Ardvorlich Burn. Head between the stone gateposts to take the estate road southwards with the burn on your right.

► At a fork, bear right to cross the burn and then, just before reaching Ardvorlich House, branch left onto a stony track. This rises gradually, passing through a gate, with the burly upper slopes of Ben Vorlich looming ahead. Continue along steeper ground, crossing two stiles as the track skirts some woodland to the left and then passes through stands of birch and oak. Already the views back across Loch Earn to Meall a' Mhadaidh and Creag Each are impressive.

► As the track forks, keep right and, after crossing a burn beside a weir, continue along what is now a path across open hillside – the gradient increasing as progress is made. The path zigzags over a slight crest, with the steepening incline taking you onto the ridge that eventually leads to the summit of Ben Vorlich.

► There are fine views of the rugged ridges of Meall na Fearna and Meall Reamhar, but be aware of steep drops into Glen Vorlich. After a final, stiff pull, the path reaches the summit trig point, with a cairn lying slightly lower to the east along a ridge.

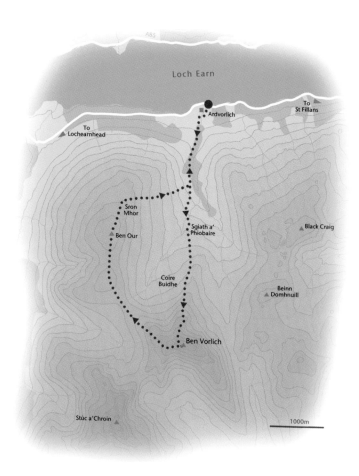

Loch Earn

To St Fillans

Ardvorlich

To Lochearnhead

Sron Mhor

Ben Our

Sgiath a'
Phiobaire

Black Craig

Coire
Buidhe

Beinn
Domhnuill

Ben Vorlich

Stùc a'Chroin

1000m

▶ For those who have had enough, simply retrace your steps to Loch Earn, but a fine, if more arduous, descent can also be enjoyed over Ben Our. From the trig point, follow a path dropping gradually west towards Bealach an Dubh Choirein, which links Ben Vorlich with neighbouring Stuc a' Chroin. Just before the path makes the sharp descent towards the bealach, bear right onto a vague path that drops steeply northwest down grassy slopes.

....

Blowing in the Wind With waters that move gradually from one end of the loch to the other, Loch Earn gives the impression of being tidal, despite its landlocked position in the heart of Highland Perthshire. In fact, this freshwater loch does have its own tidal system, but it is one created by the persistent prevailing wind – an effect known as 'seiching' – rather than any influence of the sun or the moon. As the wind blows, it applies pressure to the surface of the water, banking it up at one end of the loch before oscillation returns the water to the other end. It's an ebb and flow that is found at only one other Scottish loch – Loch Treig near Fort William – while other bodies of freshwater to experience seiching include Lake Geneva and Lake Garda.

▶ Keep an eye out for an indistinct fork where you branch left to continue the trek down to more level ground. Here, the path crosses boggy, featureless terrain, before beginning a steady ascent. When the trail soon peters out, carry on along a northwest bearing to pick up a broader grassy track that climbs a crest above Creagan nan Gabhar over to the west. The views back to Ben Vorlich are magnificent.

▶ After gaining the crest with its cairn just to the right, there's a small dip before a final, steady pull onto Ben Our, rewarded by a great view west across Loch Voil. From here, pass a small cairn to reach an obvious ridge, and descend along a narrow, sketchy path towards Sron Mhor.

▶ As Sron Mhor draws nearer, keep right and prepare to negotiate some rougher ground. Descend east down heathery slopes. Rocks underfoot make the going a little awkward while the vegetation can be quite overgrown during the summer. However, any problems are short-lived and the outbound track is soon regained. Turn left and retrace your steps to the banks of Loch Earn.

Stuc a' Chroin from Ben Vorlich

Dunalastair Water and Loch Rannoch from Schiehallion

Schiehallion

Distance 10km/6.25 miles
Time 5 hours
Start/Finish Braes of Foss car park
GR NN752558
Terrain Mountain paths and tracks.
Awkward boulderfield to cross on
summit approach
Map OS Landranger 52
Public transport Broons Service 895
from Aberfeldy and Kinloch
Rannoch can stop at Braes of Foss
road end, 3.6km from the start

Schiehallion, 'the Fairy Hill of
the Caledonians', is one of the
classic mountains of Scotland, not
least for its distinctive conical
appearance when viewed across
Loch Rannoch from the west. But
it is a slightly tougher proposition
than many first realise –
Schiehallion's upper reaches are
boulder-strewn and awkward to
cross, so extra time must be
allowed. With the mountain
standing in isolation, the views are
extensive almost from the outset,
with much flora and fauna to look
out for on the way to the top.

▶ Follow a path through a gate
at the southern end of the car park.
Turn left and continue along a
well-constructed path as it crosses
a footbridge and leads south onto
the open lower slopes of Schiehallion.

The footpath is relatively new,
created when the original, heavily-
eroded route to the summit was
realigned by the John Muir Trust,
which owns land on this eastern side
of the mountain.

▶ For much of the way, route-finding
is straightforward. Initially, the path
climbs gently but, after passing the
ruin of an old stone building, it begins
to ascend more steeply, zigzagging its
way across the heather-clad slopes.
Views of shapely Dun Coillich soon
appear to the east as do the bulky
flanks of Beinn a' Ghlo, as well as Ben
Vrackie's pointed summit beyond the
narrow length of Loch Tummel.

▶ It's a prolonged ascent, but one
made easier by the excellent path,
including several short sections of
steps. Look for the lovely shades of
pink and cream on the lichen-encrusted
rocks, while, in season, the adjacent
slopes are covered in flowering heather,
scattered patches of bogcotton and –
for those with keen eyes – arctic-alpine
species such as purple and alpine
saxifrage.

▶ Eventually at around 850m, the
path reaches a cairn which denotes a
marked change in the terrain underfoot;
here, the built path is left behind,
replaced by rocky and awkward ground.

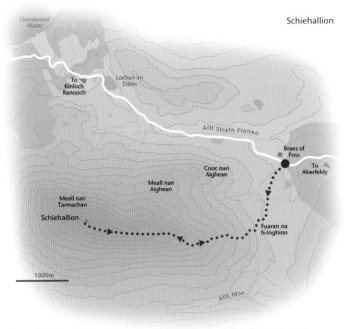

The trail swings left from the cairn and becomes less distinct as it weaves its way west along the ridge over rocks and between large boulders before disappearing altogether. It's now a case of picking your way carefully through the final boulders to reach the narrow, castellated summit some distance along the ridge.

▶ Having enjoyed the view from the summit, carefully make your way back over the boulders to rejoin the path and retrace your steps to the car park.

Weight Watchers A symmetrical mountain with a widely visible summit, Schiehallion is one of Perthshire's best-known landmarks. It also has a unique place in scientific history, having been the setting for the Reverend Nevil Maskelyne's 18th-century experiment in 'weighing the earth'. In 1774, the then Astronomer Royal became the first scientist to measure the mass of the earth, achieved by observing the deflection of a pendulum by the mass of Schiehallion. He was aided in the experiment by the mathematician Charles Hutton who first developed the concept of contour lines as a means to calculate the overall volume of Schiehallion.

Loch Tummel from Schiehallion

Kenmore Hill

Distance 4.5km/3 miles
Time 1 hour 30
Start/Finish Car park off a steep, twisting minor road, 2.4km east of Kenmore GR NN785447
Terrain Hillside and woodland paths and tracks, minor road
Map OS Landranger 52
Public transport None to start

Rugged Kenmore Hill (also known as Creag an Fhudair) rises to a height of 515m above the lochside village of Kenmore, where the River Tay begins its journey towards the North Sea. Starting off at 330m above sea level, this waymarked path climbs over lonely countryside to a high cairn with views across Perthshire. Clear paths then descend over open hillside and through woodland back to the start.

► From the car park, 500m west of Tombuie Cottage, head back along the access track to join a path that begins beside an information board. Follow the path, turning right almost immediately at a fork beside a red, blue and yellow waymarker. This walk follows red waymarkers although, slightly confusingly, the initial stages are marked only by yellow and blue ones.

► The grassy path makes a steady, meandering ascent southwest through scatterings of Scots pine and across open hillside. Cross a burn to reach a fork, going right here and following the red waymarkers. After crossing a footbridge, keep to the left of a deer fence, rising steadily over often boggy ground. The path continues over heathery slopes to reach a large cairn. Although just west of the true summit of Creag an Fhudair, the cairn provides an excellent viewpoint. Creag an Fhudair translates from Gaelic as 'Gunpowder Crag', which suggests that the land here may have been a defended hilltop or a look-out post used by local clans.

Crannog Central Loch Tay has an important underwater heritage, having once been the site of numerous crannogs – a type of ancient loch-dwelling found throughout Scotland and Ireland that dates back to the Iron Age. Usually round in structure, and built as defensive homesteads, crannogs were often symbols of wealth and power. The Scottish Crannog Centre near Kenmore features an authentic recreation of an early Iron Age loch-dwelling, built by the Scottish Trust for Underwater Archaeology. It is based on the excavation evidence from the 2500-year-old site of 'Oakbank Crannog' – one of nearly 20 crannogs to have been discovered in Loch Tay to date.

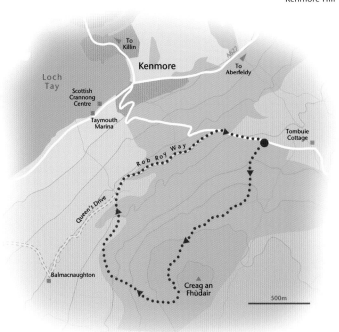

▶ Now swinging left away from the cairn, the path contours beneath the summit before gradually descending to reach a large stile over a deer fence. Cross the stile, turn left, then bear right at a waymark and drop steadily through the woodland with views along Loch Tay and the mountains beyond.

▶ This well-marked path continues the steady descent through a mixture of woodland and open countryside, contouring the steep northern slopes of Creag an Fhudair. Eventually it reaches a grassy track – an old right of way known as the Queen's Drive, and part of the Rob Roy Way.

▶ Turn right to follow the trail all the way to a gate, enjoying fine views to Kenmore and Taymouth Castle below. Once through this, turn right onto the minor road from Kenmore (still on the Rob Roy Way) and climb gently for 500m back to the car park.

Looking towards Ben Lawers from Kenmore Hill

Taymouth Castle Estate

Distance 5.5km/3.5 miles
Time 1 hour 30
Start/Finish Kenmore GR NN773454
Terrain Countryside paths and tracks
Map OS Landranger 52
Public transport Regular Stagecoach Service 892 (Aberfeldy to Kenmore and Fortingall Circular)

The River Tay flows from Loch Tay at the attractive village of Kenmore and runs east along the edge of the Taymouth Castle Estate. This walk accompanies the river, pausing at the estate's imposing 19th-century castle.

► Start from the small car park beside Loch Tay in Kenmore. Head left onto Aberfeldy Road and walk towards the village centre (The Square). Just before reaching the Kenmore Hotel, turn right and pass through the gates of Taymouth Castle Estate. As the road forks, keep right and follow the estate drive past Kenmore Primary School.

► Once around a barrier, continue through a picturesque landscape, bounded by the high wooded slopes of Drummond Hill to the north and Kenmore Hill (Creag an Fhudair) to the south. The estate drive is easily followed as it meanders northeast, passing through a golf course and a lovely pocket of woodland before turning to run parallel with a fast-flowing stretch of the Tay.

► From here, it doesn't take long to reach the imposing façade of Taymouth Castle. Pass to the right of the castle and, at the next fork, follow an attractive loop in the River Tay by heading left onto a rough track, then right onto a wide, grassy track which leads to the riverbank. Here, turn left and head upstream, keeping your eyes peeled for heron and kingfisher.

► At a crossroads, near an early 19th-century tri-arched Chinese Bridge, continue straight on through attractive birch woodland, before turning left

The Campbell Castle The present-day Taymouth Castle, which dates back to the 19th century, was built to replace the 16th-century Balloch Castle – one-time seat of the powerful Campbell Clan whose lands stretched from here to the West Coast. Having demolished the original Balloch Castle, John Campbell, the 1st Marquis of Breadalbane, set about building a far grander replacement, with final alterations made in time for the visit of Queen Victoria and Prince Albert in 1842. The building is as lavish inside as out, and includes a staircase that rises for more than 30m through all four storeys of the central tower.

at a junction to return to the estate drive. Turn left onto this to retrace your steps past the castle, coming to the fork where you looped off the main route earlier.

▶ This time turn right and carry on along the drive towards a bridge over the Allt a' Bhealaich. Just before this, turn right and take a track southwest through woods with views back over Taymouth Castle. Cross a bridge over the Allt a' Bhealaich and continue, passing a cottage and going over another bridge further on.

▶ At a fork, ignore the left-hand access track for Taymouth Sawmill to carry straight on, exiting the woodland to cross the golf course with its fine view of Ben Lawers. On reaching the estate drive, go left to return to Kenmore.

Taymouth Castle

Castle Menzies

Wade's Bridge and Castle Menzies

Distance **6.5km/4 miles**
Time **1 hour 45**
Start/Finish **The Square, Aberfeldy
GR NO856490**
Terrain **Pavement, single-track road,
riverside and woodland paths**
Map **OS Landranger 52**
Public transport **Regular Stagecoach
Service 23 between Perth and
Aberfeldy**

The River Tay flows just to the
north of Aberfeldy, passing beneath
the magnificent Wade's Bridge on
the outskirts of the town. A lovely
path travels along the Tay from
Wade's Bridge before leaving the
waterside to visit Castle Menzies
and the attractive village of Weem.
The return journey follows paths
across Aberfeldy Golf Course and
beside the Moness Burn back
into town.

▶ From the Square, follow Burnside
Lane past the tourist information centre
and turn right onto Burnside to follow
the Moness Burn. At the road end, turn
left onto Taybridge Terrace, cross the
burn, and walk past the park and the
entrance to Aberfeldy Golf Club to
reach Taybridge Road. Turn right
here and cross the ornate Wade's Bridge
(or Tay Bridge, as it's also known).

▶ Once across the bridge, take a
sharp left through a gate (signposted
for Kenmore) and join a path that leads
down to the riverside. This makes its way
along a picturesque segment of the river,
with views north to Beinn a' Ghlo. After
around 500m, branch left to a gate.
Beyond this, a signposted trail for Castle
Menzies continues alongside the Tay.

▶ At a fork, carry straight on (right) to
reach a junction. Turn right here to

Open House The name Menzies was first recorded in Scotland during the 12th
century and, as with several old Scots families, has its source in Normandy
(Mesnières, near Rouen). The earliest definitive chief of Clan Menzies was Sir Robert
de Meyneris who became Chamberlain of Scotland in 1249. His heir, Sir Alexander
Menzies, was granted the lands of Aberfeldy and Weem in around 1266, although
the current Castle Menzies dates from the 16th century, following the burning down
of the first residence of the Menzies Chiefs at Weem. During the 1745 Jacobite
uprising the castle hosted both Bonnie Prince Charlie, who rested there on his way to
Culloden, and, just days later, the Duke of Cumberland – commander of the
government forces and son of the British monarch. Rescued as a ruin in 1957 by the
Menzies Clan Society and subsequently restored, the castle and its walled garden are
now held in a charitable trust and open to the public from Easter to late-October.

follow a good path across open countryside in the direction of Weem. Beyond a gate, cross the B846, turning left along this and then right onto a side road for Castle Menzies. Detour left at a fork to follow the entrance drive to Castle Menzies, its solitary position making the building all the more striking.

► Return along the entrance drive to the fork, this time taking the other branch along a rough road. As it sweeps left, head right through a gate and walk along a narrow road lined with attractive houses, passing through a pair of stately gateposts to reach the historic village of Weem.

► Back on the B846, pass the Weem Hotel and the Old Kirk of Weem. Just before Dull & Weem Parish Church, turn left onto a minor road that climbs steeply and swings right past several houses. As the road sweeps left into Tressour Wood, bear right onto a grassy path that runs to the left of an old wall

beneath the steep slopes of the wood. The path drops gently to meet the B846 at a road junction. Go straight across here to follow this road all the way back to Wade's Bridge.

► Instead of crossing the bridge, go left through a gate onto Aberfeldy Golf Course. Initially there is no path, so just keep to the edge of the course, hugging the north bank of the Tay. In due course, a sketchy path crosses a footbridge over a burn to reach a large distinctive bridge spanning the Tay. Cross this, then take an immediate left and follow the edge of the golf course to another footbridge, this time over the Moness Burn.

► After crossing, turn right to follow a path along the burn, passing several footbridges. Just before a cottage, turn left and leave the golf course via a gate on the right. Continue straight on along Tayside Place, over Dyers Court/Market Street, and onto Chapel Street which leads back to the Square.

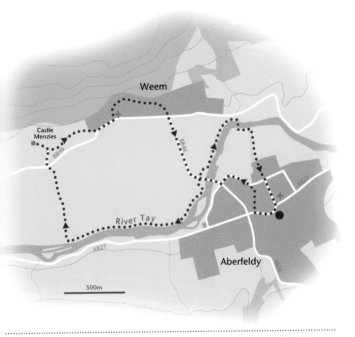

Keeping Watch General George Wade was a British military commander whose name will forever be associated with the network of military roads he had built across the Highlands. Sent to Scotland by George I in 1724 to keep an eye on the Highlanders following the 1715 Jacobite uprising, Wade recommended construction not just of roads but also of a series of barracks and bridges to help wrestle control of the Highlands. Of the 40 bridges built during this period, the magnificent Tay Bridge (or Wade's Bridge as it is more commonly known) at Aberfeldy is the most famous, and still carries traffic today. With five arches spanning the river – the bridge's central arch guarded by four obelisks – it's a surprisingly lavish structure given that it was essentially constructed for military purposes. Built in 1733 to a design by William Adam (father of the better-known Robert Adam), the bridge cost more than £4000 to complete – a hefty sum in those days.

General Wade's Bridge

Robert Burns at The Birks

The Birks of Aberfeldy

Distance 4km/2.5 miles
Time 1 hour 30
Start/Finish The Square, Aberfeldy
GR NO856490
Terrain Pavement, riverside and
woodland paths
Map OS Landranger 52
Public transport Regular Stagecoach
Service 23 between Perth and
Aberfeldy

Popularised by Robert Burns,
the woodland that clings to the
slopes around the tumbling
Moness Burn is the setting for one
of the loveliest walks in Scotland,
never mind along the River Tay.
Excellent paths hug both banks of
the burn, as numerous waterfalls
cascade through a deep gorge to
reach the Tay at Aberfeldy. The
mixed woodland that cloaks the
gorge is impressive year-round,
but particularly so in autumn.
No wonder the Bard of Ayrshire
was so inspired.

▶ From the Square, walk along
Bridgend (the A827) for about 20m
and turn left at a sign for the Birks
of Aberfeldy. This takes you through
the Aberfeldy War Memorial Archway
and onto a wooded path beside the Moness
Burn. Turn right to cross a bridge over
the burn with the path then swinging
left to continue through the wood.

▶ Many of the exotic species found
here were planted from seed in the
1960s, having been brought over from
the Himalayas and North America by
Bobby Masterton – a local vet and
keen plantsman who also created the
wonderful woodland garden at
Cluny House.

▶ At a fork, go right, cross another
bridge and climb a flight of steps.
After a few more steps, turn right
through a gap in a wall onto Crieff
Road. Head straight across the road,
then bear left to cross Urlar Road and
join the signposted Birks path.

From Birks to Burns *Birks* is Scots for 'birch trees' which, together with oak, ash
and willow, make up a significant portion of this woodland – one of the finest in all
of Perthshire's Big Tree Country. Not surprisingly, it is home to a host of wildlife,
particularly birds, with green and great-spotted woodpecker, treecreeper, flycatcher,
dipper and sparrowhawk among the many species to be seen and heard here.
Much of the gorge is now designated as a Site of Special Scientific Interest for its
rich plant and animal life. Originally known as the Den of Moness, the woodland
was renamed following a visit by Robert Burns in 1787 which inspired the
subsequent penning of his song 'The Birks of Aberfeldie'.

► Continue past The Moness Stone, an example of a prehistoric cup-marked stone that was moved to this site in 2005, having first been excavated nearby in the 1960s. The path bears right just before the Birks lower car park and climbs gradually past the upper car park. Continue straight on and follow a broad woodland track into the Birks.

► Take the right branch at a fork and follow the path as it climbs steeply south, taking you high above the west bank of the Moness Burn. Even at this early point in the walk, the surroundings are extremely impressive. Eventually the path turns left over a footbridge to cross a feeder burn and then runs to the right of a fence – the drops here are almost vertical and there are great views of the gorge.

► Continue to a flight of steps on the left. Walk down these to cross a bridge overlooking the Moness Falls, which drop vertically into the yawning chasm beneath. At the end of the bridge, the path sweeps right, then left onto the east side of the gorge.

► After climbing a flight of steps, there are more spectacular views of the falls before the path drops gradually, passing a line from Robert Burns' song, 'The Birks of Aberfeldie'. Steeper sections zigzag down steps into the gorge with 'the crystal streamlet' of the Moness Burn below. The path passes the natural stone seat where Burns is said to have rested during a visit in 1787 while, further down, you'll encounter a statue of the Bard himself.

► A gentler walk now ensues with the path running alongside the water to soon reach a footbridge. Cross this and turn right onto the outbound path to retrace your steps to Aberfeldy.

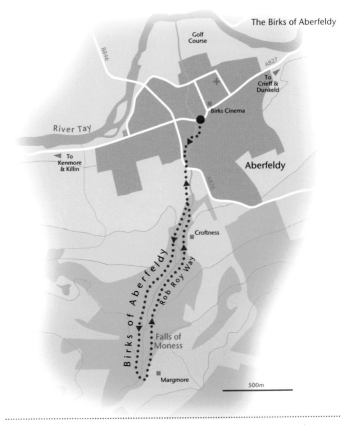

A Distilled History Aberfeldy is a small but busy town, built around its market square. The town developed greatly following construction of the magnificent Tay Bridge (General Wade's Bridge) in 1733, with industries such as cotton milling and, in particular, whisky distilling coming to the fore. The area has a long history of distilling (both legal and otherwise) with sites at nearby Grantully and Aberfeldy's own Pittiely Distillery which closed in 1867. It was replaced by Aberfeldy Distillery which is now home to Dewar's World of Whisky, one of the town's main visitor attractions.

Ben Vrackie

Distance 9km/5.5 miles
Time 3 hours 30
Start/Finish Car park 800m north of Moulin Inn GR NN945598
Terrain Hill and mountain paths and tracks. One steep ascent and descent
Map OS Landranger 52
Public transport Regular Scotrail Service from Glasgow, Edinburgh and Inverness to Pitlochry or Citylink Service M91 from Edinburgh and Inverness to Pitlochry, leaving around 1.5km to the start

A familiar landmark that rises to a height of 841m above the former spa town of Pitlochry, Ben Vrackie has an excellent and mostly gentle main path as far as the pretty Loch a' Choire, where a steep pull then takes you to the craggy summit. It is a particularly good choice of hill for younger walkers, with rewarding views sweeping across the Cairngorms massif and much of the Central Highlands.

► From the Ben Vrackie car park, follow a well-marked path through woodland as it climbs north alongside the Moulin Burn. In due course, the path merges with a track coming in from the right. Continue straight on, following the path over a bridge and through a gate to emerge onto open moorland.

► The path begins to climb steadily, heading north and then northeast with fine views opening up northwards towards the summit of Ben Vrackie and south along the Rivers Tummel and Tay. Stick to the main path, ignoring a branch off to the left, to continue between the craggy outcrops of Creag Bhreac and Meall na h-Aodainn Moire.

► Once through another gate, the path bears north to reach the secluded Loch a' Choire. This is a lovely spot to enjoy the moorland surroundings before negotiating the final steep path to the summit, visible ahead.

Speckled View The Scottish landscape is littered with hills translating from the Gaelic *Beinn Bhreac* ('Speckled Hill'), but Ben Vrackie is probably the best known. Classified as a Corbett (a Scottish mountain between 2500 and 2999 feet), its close proximity to Pitlochry and excellent path make it very popular with walkers. However, it is the outlook from the summit that sets Ben Vrackie apart from many of its namesakes. Distant views include the peaks of Glenshee and the Cairngorms to the north, Ben Lawers to the southwest and Ben Alder to the west, but the striking outline of Beinn a' Ghlo's three Munros is perhaps the most memorable.

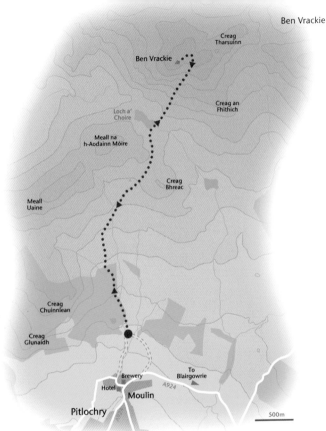

Creag Tharsuinn

Ben Vrackie

Creag an Fhithich

Loch a' Choire

Meall na h-Aodainn Mòire

Creag Bhreac

Meall Uaine

Creag Chuinnlean

Creag Glunaidh

Brewery

To Blairgowrie

Hotel

Moulin

A924

Pitlochry

500m

► Carry on along the near shore of the loch, crossing the outlet burn on stepping stones to reach the start of the summit path. This takes the form of steep zigzags – a tough pull with Loch a' Choire growing ever smaller when you glance back – but the summit is soon reached, with the trig point sitting a little to the west.

► Once you've soaked up the views from the top, retrace your steps to Loch a' Choire and back along the outbound path to the start.

Beinn a' Ghlo from Ben Vrackie

River Tay from Birnam Hill

Black Linn at The Hermitage

Birnam, Rumbling Bridge and The Hermitage

Distance 10km/6.25 miles
Time 3 hours
**Start/Finish Perth Road, Birnam
GR NO032418**
**Terrain Riverside, woodland paths,
countryside paths and tracks and
single-track road**
Map OS Landranger 52
**Public transport Regular Scotrail
Service from Glasgow and Inverness
to Birnam. Regular Stagecoach
Service 23 from Perth and Aberfeldy
to Birnam**

**Much of the countryside around the
village of Birnam is cloaked in
wildlife-rich woodland that makes
for a wonderful mix of red, brown
and orange during the autumn
months. This walk visits The
Hermitage and Rumbling Bridge –
both renowned for their autumnal
hues – while the River Braan and its
many spectacular falls add to the
route's appeal. Throw in some truly
ancient trees, including one of the
tallest in Britain, plus the legend of
Ossian, and this is a walk with plenty
to intrigue and entertain.**

► Follow Birnam Glen road (signposted
'Inchewan Path') from opposite the
Birnam Hotel on Perth Road, and pass
beneath the busy A9. Head towards

Dunkeld & Birnam Railway Station,
bearing left just before the railway
bridge to follow a rough, stony path
under the line to a crossroads. Go
straight across, then right at a fork to
drop down through a gate into
woodland. From here, a lovely wide
path climbs gently southwest beside the
Inchewan Burn in the company of
rowan, beech and ash.

► After around 1.6km, the path reaches
a fork. Go right, cross a bridge over the
Inchewan Burn and continue to a
junction, turning left here. At the next
junction, head right onto a signposted
forestry track for Inver Car Park. This
leads through the Ladywell Plantation to
a junction where you go right onto
another track. Descend gradually to
reach a choice of paths, here taking the
signposted Braan Path to Rumbling
Bridge (first left).

► This rises through conifer woodland
to meet a path on the right, marked
'Inchewan Braan Paths'. Take this
through a gate and across a footbridge
to meander through deciduous
woodland, passing to the left of a
cottage, which lies south of
Dundonnachie, and crossing another
footbridge. When you meet a track,
turn left and walk through birch

woodland, emerging over a stile into open country with views towards Craig Vinean.

▶ The track continues southwest through open countryside (keep dogs on leads) past a house at Tomgarrow to reach a junction. Turn right and walk down a narrow road to the A822. Across the road, a woodland path leads you onwards and over a footbridge. Bear left at a fork and cross another bridge to a viewpoint high above Rumbling Bridge and the River Braan – a spot said to have greatly impressed Queen Victoria when she visited in 1865. At the next fork, go right to head down to a narrow road where you turn right to cross Rumbling Bridge.

▶ When the road bends sharply to the left, go through a gate on the right for The Hermitage. The path drops gently to a gate and crosses a footbridge to meet a waymarked trail on the right which leads through glorious woodland. At the next fork, take the right branch to follow a path above the River Braan. A right turn at the next fork leads to the impressive Ossian's Hall at The Hermitage and views of the spectacular Black Linn.

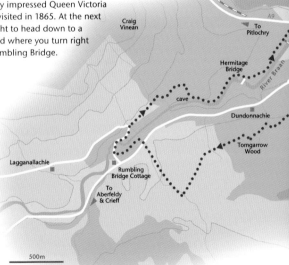

▶ Keeping the Braan to your right, follow the path away from The Hermitage, turning right at the next fork to pass beneath a railway arch and reach a car park. Once through the car park, and just before the A9, bear right onto a path and then right onto a narrow road at a sign for Inver/ Birnam/Dunkeld. Follow this road through Inver before turning left along a path which passes a Forestry Commission car park. This takes you to a bridge over the Braan just beside an underpass.

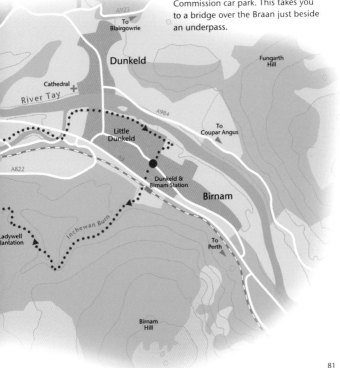

► Cross the bridge, then head under the A9, immediately turning left onto a path that reaches the River Tay at the outflow of the Braan. The route now accompanies the Tay on its journey downstream, passing beneath Thomas Telford's stately Dunkeld Bridge and encountering the ancient Birnam Oak – thought to be a remnant from the Birnam Forest made famous by William Shakespeare's tragedy *Macbeth* – and the somewhat younger but equally impressive Birnam Sycamore.

► After passing these trees, turn right up some steps onto a path for Birnam. Where the path ends, bear right onto a road which returns you to Perth Road.

Creative Endeavours The sweeping woodland of the Hermitage may look natural, but this is very much a planned landscape – the work of the Dukes of Atholl whose main residence was (and remains) at Blair Castle, but who maintained a winter retreat at nearby Dunkeld House. Perhaps the most spectacular of the many trees planted along the banks of the River Braan is a Douglas fir which, when measured in 2009, topped out at 61m high, making it the fourth largest tree in the UK. But the Dukes built in stone as well as wood, with the Hermitage viewing pavilion constructed in 1757 to frame the views over the raging Black Linn Falls becoming a major draw for the great and good of the day. William and Dorothy Wordsworth, the painter John Turner and composer Felix Mendelssohn all paid a visit. It was around this time that another visitor, the Scottish poet James Macpherson, announced that he had discovered the ancient poems of the Gaelic bard Ossian (son of Fingal) and translated them into English – although it is now thought he wrote the poems himself. Nevertheless, the Dukes of Atholl were only too happy to exploit the story, renaming the Hermitage as Ossian's Hall and creating an artificial cave which became known as Ossian's Cave.

Countryside near Rumbling Bridge

Lomond Hills from Birnam

Birnam Hill

Distance 6.25km/4 miles
Time 2 hours 30
Start/Finish Perth Road, Birnam
GR NO032418
Terrain Hill and countryside paths
and tracks, single-track road. One
steep ascent/descent
Map OS Landranger 52
Public transport Regular Scotrail
Service from Glasgow and Inverness
to Birnam. Regular Stagecoach
Service 23 from Perth and Aberfeldy
to Birnam

**Although Birnam Hill only just
scrapes the 400m mark, it
nonetheless offers a spectacular
vantage point from which to enjoy
the surrounding landscape.**

▶ From almost directly opposite the
Birnam Hotel on Perth Road, join
Birnam Glen road (signposted
'Inchewan Path') and follow it beneath
the A9 and past Dunkeld & Birnam
Railway Station. Just before the railway
bridge, bear left and follow a rough,
stony path that passes beneath the
railway line to reach a crossroads. Head
straight across this, then go left at a fork
to follow a wooded path as it climbs
gradually to a signpost for Birnam Hill.

▶ Turn left onto a solid path, which
zigzags steeply up Birnam Hill's wooded
slopes. At a fork, take either path as
both continue to rise steeply, eventually
meeting a little below a craggy outcrop.
Carry on past the outcrop or detour left
onto the path which climbs easily to its
top – here, you can pause to enjoy the
fine views along the Tay to peaks such as
Deuchary Hill, just north of Dunkeld,
and Ben Vrackie, by Pitlochry. Return
the same way.

▶ Back on the main path, follow a
meandering route south through
heather and woodland, eventually
bearing left where a final short but
steep climb gains the top of Birnam Hill,
also known as the King's Seat.

....

Warrior Hill A fine cairn adorns the summit of Birnam Hill, where the views extend
northwest to the eye-catching cone of Schiehallion, east along the meandering Tay
and across the flatter plains of Perthshire to Fife and the Lomond Hills. Birnam
translates from Old English as 'Village of the Warrior'. A hill and village name with
an English origin may seem unusual in the heart of the Highlands, but during the
12th century the lands around Birnam and Dunkeld were subject to feudalism by
English kings. Much later, the coming of the railway in 1856 saw Birnam become a
popular holiday spot for well-to-do Victorians, including Beatrix Potter whose family
made regular visits here from their home in the Lake District.

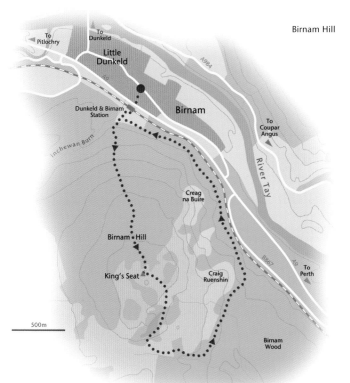

► Continue past the cairn and along the 'Path to Quarry Car Park'. Once over a little crag, drop down over open hillside with views across to Fife. A steady descent soon takes you to a flight of steps, which drop steeply. The twists and turns of the path continue southwards, traversing Birnam Hill's lower slopes.

► In due course, bear left and drop back into woodland, eventually reaching a track. Turn left for Birnam and continue for around 150m before bearing right onto a path that undulates through woodland, crossing a couple of footbridges before running parallel with the A9.

► Turn right when a broader track merges from the left, heading past some houses onto a narrow road to return to the outbound route. Turn right to retrace your steps to Birnam.

River Tay and Dunkeld Bridge

Dunkeld Cathedral

Dunkeld and Loch of the Lowes

Distance **9.5km/6 miles**
Time **3 hours 30**
Start/Finish **Atholl Street Car Park
(charge), Dunkeld GR NO026429**
Terrain **Riverbank, woodland and
countryside paths and tracks.
Single-track road**
Map **OS Landranger 52**
Public transport **Regular Scotrail
Service from Glasgow and Inverness
to Dunkeld/Birnam. Regular Citylink
Service M91 from Edinburgh and
Inverness to Dunkeld**

A range of walks follow the Tay from
the centre of the historic town of
Dunkeld. One of the very best heads
out to nearby Loch of the Lowes
which is renowned for its breeding
ospreys and abundance of other
wildlife. This walk also visits the
magnificent Dunkeld Cathedral.

► From Atholl Street Car Park,
turn right onto Atholl Street and
walk through Dunkeld, turning right
again onto High Street. Keep to the
right of the large fountain at The Cross
and head through an archway to
access Stanley Hill, an area of parkland
(also known as Schoochie Hill) that
was created by the Second Duke of
Atholl around 1730. Turn left at a
junction and walk through the park
to a fork.

► Dunkeld Cathedral (free to visit,
donations welcome) is off to the left
and well worth exploring before
returning to the fork and bearing left.
Go left at two further forks to reach the
River Tay. Continue west along one of
the finest stretches of this river, the
banks cloaked in woodland, with views
back to the stately Dunkeld Bridge.

On Religious Grounds Dunkeld became Scotland's religious centre in the 9th
century when St Columba's relics were relocated here from Iona to keep them safe
from Viking raids. For centuries, the focal point was Dunkeld Cathedral, an impressive
structure built in stages between 1260 and 1501 on the site of a previous monastery.
The cathedral is dedicated to St Columba and it is thought a variety of associated
relics are buried beneath the chancel. Having previously been damaged during the
Reformation in 1560 – when anything deemed 'Popish' was destroyed – the
Cathedral suffered much worse during the first Jacobite uprising. Following their
victory at the Battle of Killiecrankie in 1689, Jacobite forces attacked government
troops based at Dunkeld in a battle that saw the cathedral and much of the town
burnt down. Many of the buildings in the town today date from after that time, with
most visitors arriving via the Thomas Telford-designed Dunkeld Bridge, which finally
linked Dunkeld with neighbouring Birnam when completed in 1809.

1000m

► After a while, the path brings you to a track which leads to the luxury Hilton Dunkeld House Hotel. Bear left onto the entrance drive and then, just before the hotel itself, branch right to skirt round the back of it and through a car park. At the next fork, keep right and climb away from the hotel to a road. Cross this, turn right and then go left through a gate onto an Atholl Woods path that passes tranquil Polney Loch – its shores fringed by trees that put on their best show in autumn.

► At the far end of the loch, bear right and continue through Atholl Estates woodland to reach Cally Car Park. From here, follow a broad track (signposted for Loch of the Lowes), continuing straight on at the next crossroads to reach a waymarked path on the right. Take this path, descending almost to the A923 but branching left just before you reach it to head through attractive beech woodland and meet the road further east, opposite Dunkeld and Birnam Golf Course.

▶ Cross the A923 and follow the golf course access road past the clubhouse to the car park. At its right corner, join a path that turns left before heading through a gate onto a field-edge path. Continue straight on through two more gates to follow a road past some cottages at Fungarth, where a rougher track drops down through scenic countryside before climbing to a junction. Take the left turn and follow a track above the golf course, passing through two gates along the way, to reach a minor road. Cross here and head left along a path that leads to the Scottish Wildlife Trust's Loch of the Lowes visitor centre and hides.

▶ Once you've looked for that elusive osprey or pine marten, retrace your steps to the junction just a little southeast of Fungarth. Take the left fork (signposted for Dunkeld) to follow a grassy path. Pass through a gate and bear right onto a broad track, which descends steeply at one point to veer right onto a narrow road. Follow this to Brae Street on the outskirts of Dunkeld. Turn right and walk along this quiet road, which eventually drops steeply back into town at Atholl Street. Turn right to return to the car park.

Reproduction Line Much of Loch of the Lowes is a wildlife reserve run by the Scottish Wildlife Trust. Together with the neighbouring Loch of Craiglush and Loch of Butterstone, it is a haven for an assortment of wildlife, with the loch's pair of breeding ospreys a magnet for visitors. The birds winter in West Africa, but are resident from early-April to late-August, with their comings and goings easily enjoyed thanks to a variety of observation hides, as well as webcams that record action from inside the nest. The return of ospreys – the birds were persecuted to extinction in Scotland almost a century ago – is a major conservation success story and there are now thought to be around 240 breeding pairs in Scotland. The Scottish Wildlife Trust's visitor centre at Loch of the Lowes is a great place to learn more – not just about ospreys but also the many other species that make their homes here.

Polney Loch

Perth and the River Tay

The Tay from Smeaton's Bridge

Perth City

Distance 5.75km/3.5 miles
Time 1 hour 30
Start/Finish Perth Railway Station
GR NO113232
Terrain Lochside and parkland paths
and tracks
Map OS Landranger 58
Public transport Regular trains
and buses from all major Scottish
cities to Perth. Regular Scottish
Citylink Service M8 from Glasgow
and Dundee to Perth and Service
M91 from Edinburgh and Inverness
to Perth

Straddling the banks of the River Tay,
Perth is a great place to spend a few
hours with an enticing mix of culture,
architecture and history that belies
its relatively small size. Easy going
throughout, this walk visits many of
the city's finest buildings and areas
of historical interest.

► From Perth Railway Station, follow
King's Place onto Marshall Place and
then turn left at the river onto Tay
Street beside the Fergusson Gallery –
a quirky building that celebrates the
life and work of John Duncan
Fergusson and his wife, the modern
dance pioneer Margaret Morris. Born
in Leith in 1874, Fergusson's parents
were from Pitlochry and he considered
Perthshire to be his home. Friends
with Picasso and Matisse, he is
regarded as one of the most influential
Scottish artists of the 20th century.

► Continue under a railway bridge
and along the riverfront, here lined
with a variety of handsome buildings.
Turn left onto Canal Street and
continue past Greyfriars Church and
Burial Ground. The earliest
gravestones in the cemetery date from
1580, although many more would

Seventh Heaven Granted city status – Scotland's seventh – in 2012 to mark the
Queen's Diamond Jubilee, Perth also celebrated (in 2010) the 800th anniversary of
being granted a Royal Burgh Charter by King William 'The Lion' of Scotland.
However, Perth's history dates back much further than that. Its importance was
established in 83AD when the Romans built a fort at the nearby confluence of the
Rivers Tay and Almond. Kenneth MacAlpin, King of Scots, arrived in 843AD at the
old Pictish capital of Scone to establish a nation and a Royal Seat. King David I
continued Perth's development in the 12th century, with its river location helping
Perth become a thriving port and market centre. By the 14th century, it was
acknowledged by the staple port of Bruges (the 'staple' being a system of trade and
taxation within Europe at the time) as one of Scotland's four great towns, alongside
Edinburgh, Aberdeen and Dundee.

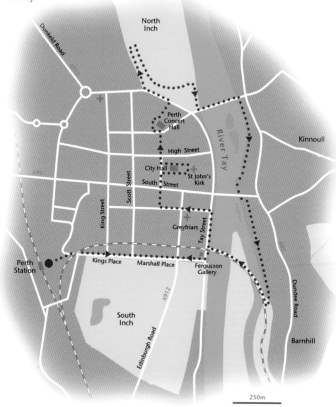

The Tay

North Inch

Dunkeld Road

Perth Concert Hall

River Tay

Kinnoull

High Street

City Hall

South Street

St John's Kirk

Scott Street

King Street

Greyfriars

Tay Street

Kings Place

Marshall Place

Fergusson Gallery

Perth Station

South Inch

Edinburgh Road

Dundee Road

Barnhill

250m

have survived had Oliver Cromwell and his troops not plundered them following the capture of Perth in 1651. At the southern end of the cemetery sit 13 of the very earliest gravestones, all in remarkably good condition.

► Cross Princess Street and then, just after a car park, turn right onto Ropemakers Close – originally used by ropemakers as a 'ropewalk' during the twisting process. Follow this lane to South Street, continue straight across onto King Edward Street and then take the first right, at Perth City Hall, onto St John's Place. Follow this to the historic St John's Kirk.

► Head left around the front of the church onto St John Street, and then left again where St John's Place leads back to King Edward Street. Turn right here, cross over High Street and walk along another lane that leads to Mill Street. Turn left, then right after a pelican crossing onto a pedestrianised walkway. Bear right onto North Port Lane and walk past the striking contemporary architecture of Perth Concert Hall and what was once the site of Perth Castle.

► At Charlotte Street (A989), turn left to soon reach the elegant Rose Terrace at the edge of North Inch park on your right. Follow this row of Georgian town houses as far as Perth's Old Academy, built in 1804 by Robert Reid, with a clock and Britannia statue added later. Opposite the Academy building, enter North Inch where the Battle of the Clans took place in 1396 – a staged event instigated by King Robert III to settle a long-running feud between two warring clans. The result was predictably bloody.

► Turn right to skirt the perimeter of the park on a path which curves back towards the River Tay. Bear left at a statue to go through some gateposts and then turn right after the war memorials. Now beside the river, pass through an arch of Perth Bridge (also known as Smeaton's Bridge) to rejoin Tay Street where you turn right to cross the bridge.

► Once on the other side, walk down a few steps on your right to Commercial Street and head right down the first flight of steps you come to, turning left at the bottom to soon join a lovely riverside path. Continue right at the next two forks to eventually pass through an arch beneath Queen's Bridge.

► Turn left here to climb steps into Rodney Gardens. Following the garden trail clockwise will return you to the riverside path, where you turn left and continue to a fork. Make a right here and again at the next fork to cross Bellwood Park to a pedestrian bridge. Turn right to head back over the river next to the railway line and, at the end of the bridge, walk down a flight of steps to reach Tay Street again. From here, turn left, then right onto Marshall Place to return to the station.

South Inch

South Inch and Craigie Hill

Distance 7km/4.25 miles
Time 1 hour 45
Start/Finish Perth Railway Station
GR NO113232
Terrain Pavement, parkland and
woodland path and tracks
Map OS Landranger 58
Public transport Regular trains
and buses from all major Scottish
cities to Perth. Regular Scottish
Citylink Service M8 from Glasgow
and Dundee and Service M91
from Edinburgh and Inverness
to Perth

Perth is the birthplace of William
Soutar, one of Scotland's finest
poets. Although bedridden for a
large part of his adult life, Soutar
played happily in the parkland
and woodland in and around
Perth during his younger years
and wrote extensively about this
experience throughout his life.
This scenic route visits some of the
places enjoyed by Soutar and which
inspired much of his work.

► From Perth Railway Station, follow
King's Place onto Marshall Place and
then to Tay Street beside the Fergusson
Gallery. Turn right and walk along a
path through the parkland of South Inch
alongside Shore Road.

► Follow the path past a skate park
and then swing right just before some
buildings. Here a single-track road
follows the edge of South Inch to
reach a junction at Edinburgh Road
(A912). Turn left along the A912, cross
the road and then turn right onto a
path, which runs between South Inch
and South Inch Terrace, the birthplace
of William Soutar.

► At a crossroads, turn left to leave
South Inch, passing beneath a railway
arch, then along a path by the Craigie
Burn. Some steps lead onto Glenearn
Road. Cross over onto Windsor Terrace
and then, just before Millburn Court,
turn left up a passage, which climbs a
flight of steps. Follow this as it swings
right and then left onto Moncreiffe

South Inch Stronghold South Inch is a beautiful rectangle of parkland that today
is popular with locals and visitors alike. It used to be the site of an artillery fort and
barracks built by Oliver Cromwell's troops when they occupied Perth in 1651
following the Battle of Dunbar. Known as Cromwell's Citadel, this vast defensive
fortification was partially demolished a decade later with the restoration of the
monarchy and the subsequent return of Charles II from his French exile. The citadel
was re-fortified briefly during the Jacobite risings of 1715 and 1745, but nothing
remains visible today, its foundations lying hidden beneath the turf.

Terrace. At the top of this road, turn right and immediately right again onto Moredun Terrace, which soon swings left onto Verena Terrace with fine views opening out over Perth.

► Turn right onto Craigie Knowes Road, then left at the top to climb Glenlochay Road. At a bend sweeping left down to Glendevon Road, take the side road continuing uphill. After a very short distance, a gate on the right gives access to a rough farm track contouring the edge of Craigie Hill community woodland. This climbs gradually with views to Kinnoull Hill and the Tay. William Soutar played here regularly as a youngster.

► The farm track soon runs to the left of Craigie Hill Golf Course, descending gently to a fork. Go right here and drop down through Buckie Braes woodland, which runs alongside the Buckie Burn. This is another of Soutar's favourite spots, captured in one of his poems: 'Monie a bairn frae our toun Haiks up to the Buckie Braes'.

► After skirting around a ravine, the path descends to the foot of the braes, exiting the woodland onto a single-track road. Follow this past several houses to a junction, turning right to make your way past the entrance to Craigie Hill Golf Club.

► Continue along a woodland path, go through a gate and, beyond several more houses, take the middle path at a three-way fork. Follow this to Craigie View. Turn left here and, at the roundabout, go left again to walk all the way down Craigie Knowes Road.

The Perth Poet Born in 1898, William Soutar is regarded as one of the finest poets Scotland has ever produced. His early years were spent in Perth, drawing inspiration from its history and landscape, and he was educated at Perth Academy. Soutar served in the Royal Navy during World War I, but was sent home on sick leave in 1918 – the start of an adult life characterised by illness. He studied English Literature at Edinburgh, and had high hopes for a career in teaching, but by his mid-20s poor health saw him back living with his parents in Wilson Street, Perth. He was eventually diagnosed with incurable arthritis of the spine. Although bedridden from the age of 32, Soutar wrote continuously, with his greatest legacy being the poetry written in Scots, including works such as 'John Knox', 'Ae Simmer's Day' and 'Craigie Knowes'. He was friends with Hugh MacDiarmid and Neil Gunn, and received regular visits from many notable Scottish writers. In July 1943, Soutar was diagnosed with tuberculosis and died in October of that year, aged 45.

▶ At the roundabout at the bottom of the hill, turn right onto Queen Street, passing some fine houses to reach Glenearn Road. Turn right, then left to rejoin the outbound path along the Craigie Burn. Once through the railway arch and back into South Inch, head diagonally across the open park to reach Marshall Place. Turn left and retrace your steps to the railway station.

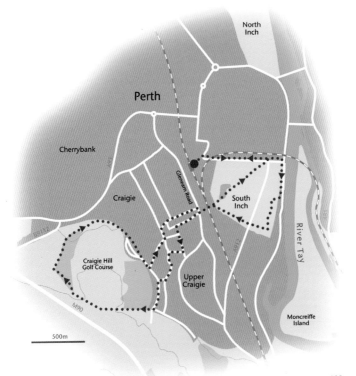

The Tay from Kinnoull Hill

Kinnoull Hill

Distance 8.5km/5.25 miles
Time 2 hours
Start/Finish Perth Railway Station
GR NO113232
Terrain Pavement, woodland path
and tracks
Map OS Landranger 58
Public transport Regular trains
and buses from all major Scottish
cities to Perth. Regular Scottish
Citylink Service M8 from Glasgow
and Dundee and Service M91 from
Edinburgh and Inverness to Perth

Providing a dramatic backdrop to
the city, the woodland park of
Kinnoull Hill rises prominently above
Perth. A walk from the city centre
through the woods to its summit
offers great wildlife-spotting
opportunities, as well as the chance
to enjoy the views along the River
Tay, which meanders leisurely around
the base of the hill.

► From Perth Railway Station, join
King's Place and follow it onto Marshall
Place to the junction with Tay Street.
Head left to walk beside the River Tay,
turning right onto South Street to cross
the river.

► Turn right onto Dundee Street,
then left onto Manse Road, which
begins a gradual climb to a mini-
roundabout. Continue, using the verge
when the pavement ends, as far as a
second roundabout, where you turn
right onto Hatton Road. Follow this on
a sustained climb through leafy
suburbs, eventually swinging left onto
Corsie Hill Road.

► At a small car park, turn right
and ascend a steep, grassy path to a
view indicator on Corsie Hill. Before
the opening of Perth Bridge in 1770,
the village of Corsiehill was a meeting
place for smugglers who tried to avoid
paying the taxes of Perth. The site offers

Woodland Wonderland Gifted to the Town Council of Perth by Lord Dewar in
1924, Kinnoull Hill became Scotland's first woodland park in 1991. The park also
encompasses the land around neighbouring Deuchny Hill, later acquired from the
Kinfauns Estate by the Forestry Commission. During its private ownership, Kinnoull
Hill was part of a carefully-planned landscape laid out for ladies and gentlemen of
a certain class to enjoy this peaceful, beautiful spot. Today, the whole park is
managed through a partnership of landowners and the local community, with its
network of paths accessible to all. Walk quietly through this mixed woodland, and
you may well spot a range of wildlife, including red squirrel, roe deer and
peregrine falcon.

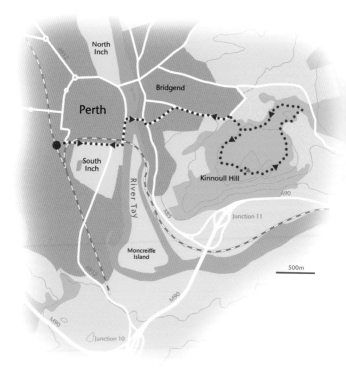

views that extend to Ben More, Stob Binnein, Ben Vorlich and the southern Cairngorms.

▶ Continue to climb past a green marker to a blue waymarked path on the right. Follow this as it descends

gradually through mixed woodland, in time bearing left to reach a crossroads. Go straight on, with the path meandering through pinewood to a junction. Turn left and climb through woodland, bearing left at a fork. From here, it's a simple and rather beautiful walk with the gradient steepening slightly to reach a path on the left signposted for Kinnoull summit.

► After a steady ascent, the path sweeps right to a great viewpoint, although you'll need to take a further path on the left to reach Kinnoull Hill's summit trig point. The views extend west across the flat plains of Perthshire to the big mountains of the Southern and Central Highlands. Be aware, however, there are steep cliffs all around, so care is needed.

► From the trig point, follow the path down to the right and back into woodland. After about 30m, look for an often muddy path on the right. Take this path as it undulates its way to a junction, where you turn right to reach the dramatically-positioned Kinnoull Tower. Sitting precariously on the edge of a sheer crag, this Victorian folly is said to be a copy of the watchtowers found along the Rhine.

► At the tower, head east along a path that runs close to the cliff edge before swinging sharply left to a junction. Turn right and follow the path as it descends gradually through beech woodland – at its best in its autumn finery – and then left of a field. At a fork, head right and follow the now fenced field-edge path, skirting Kinnoull Hill woodland, down to a gate.

► Turn left at a signpost for Corsiehill car park and, beyond another gate, follow a broad track through mostly Scots pine and birch woodland. At a fork, take the left path, which soon begins to climb steadily to a path on the right, again signposted for the car park. Follow this path as it crosses a footbridge and exits the woodland. Turn right to shortly rejoin the outbound path, return to Corsie Hill and retrace your steps to Perth.

Perth from Kinnoull Hill

Kinnoull Hill from Moncreiffe

Moncreiffe Hill

Distance 4km/2.5 miles
Time 1 hour 15
Start/Finish Tay Car Park, Rhynd, near Tarsappie GR NN135210
Terrain Woodland path and tracks
Map OS Landranger 58
Public transport Stagecoach Services 35A, 36 & 56 from Perth Bus Station to Rhynd Road, 1.25km from the start point

Rising above the south bank of the River Tay on the outskirts of Perth, the heavily-wooded Moncreiffe Hill is blessed with a rich cultural as well as natural history, with two Pictish forts around its summit. The site is cared for by the Woodland Trust and an excellent selection of paths and tracks provide access to both forts – offering panoramic views across much of Perthshire, as well as sculptures to look out for along the way. This route follows the white waymarked trail.

► From the Woodland Trust's Tay Car Park, head through a gate onto a good path which passes through a second gate before beginning a steady zigzag up the lower slopes of Moncreiffe Hill.

► Once past *The Portal* (a timber circle that symbolises the area's many hill forts), continue through a gate to climb, gently at first, to a fork. Head left here

and make the steady, clockwise climb, passing some of the wooden sculptures that are dotted around the woodland.

► Stick to the main track, which soon swings right to a junction. Go left here at which point the gradient eases a little. At a fork, bear left onto a path signed for Moredun Hill Fort and walk a short distance to an information board. Here, there are two paths on the left: one steep, one less so. Both can be climbed onto Moredun and the broad summit of Moncreiffe Hill with its great views.

► Particularly prominent are the twin peaks of Fife's Lomond Hills to the southeast, while the aspect to the north is dominated by some of the Central Highlands' big mountains. However, the view across the snaking River Tay to the craggy, wooded slopes of Kinnoull Hill is the most striking of all.

► Return to the base of the fort, turn right and retrace your steps to the main track. Once there, turn left onto the white waymarked route signposted for Moncreiffe Hill Fort.

► At the next information board, turn left and climb a short distance to the hill fort. Trees restrict the view north, but this is compensated by views to the south that extend to Bridge of Earn and along Strathearn towards the Ochil Hills.

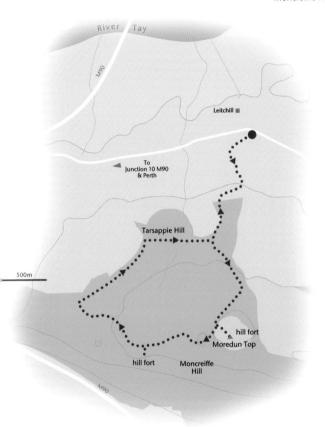

► Retrace your steps to the main track and turn left to wander along an easy path through mixed woodland to a fork. Go right here and continue for approximately 500m past a green waymarked track on the right to reach a second track, also on the right. Follow this as it climbs back to the outbound path on the left. Take this to return to the car park.

Bridge of Earn from Moncreiffe

Camperdown, Templeton and Clatto Parks

Distance 8.25km/5.25 miles
Time 2 hours 30
Start/Finish Camperdown Park,
Dundee GR NO360325
Terrain Pavement, woodland and
parkland paths and tracks
Map OS Landranger 54
Public transport Regular trains and
buses from across Scotland to
Dundee. Regular Stagecoach Service
57 from Seagate Bus Station to
Camperdown Park entrance

Dundee is the largest settlement by the River Tay and Camperdown House is the centrepiece of its biggest public park, situated on the outskirts of the city and comprising three country parks. This walk enjoys good paths and delightful sections of woodland throughout.

► From the car park by Camperdown House, head for the main drive which swings right towards the house. Turn left, and walk past the front of the house to a wooden starting hut by the golf course. After passing the hut, turn left onto a pink waymarked path which makes its way through woodland to the right of the golf course.

► Continue straight on at the first crossroads, right at the next junction

and then straight over again at another crossroads. Immediately bear left onto a blue/green waymarked path (at a sign for the 2nd tee). Follow this around a barrier and through lovely woodland where wood sorrel, red campion and wood anemone thrive in spring and summer.

► The path climbs gently, in due course crossing a track beside a cottage. Continue around a further barrier to pass another blue/green waymarker. At the next marker, bear left onto an indistinct path and follow this to the A923, leaving Camperdown Country Park. Cross the main road, turn left and follow the pavement to Birkhill, turning right onto Blairfield Road. Once past a pub and car park, turn right through a gap in a hedge and bear left to join a path that runs through Birkhill Woodland, alongside Blairfield Road.

► At a junction, head right, then left at a fork where the path now skirts the edge of the wood with great views of the Sidlaw Hills. Cross a minor road and bear right into Templeton Woods where a yellow waymarked path meanders through the trees. Keep an eye out for red squirrels, roe deer and the elusive (but noisy) jay. Continue straight on at a fork and then, once over a small

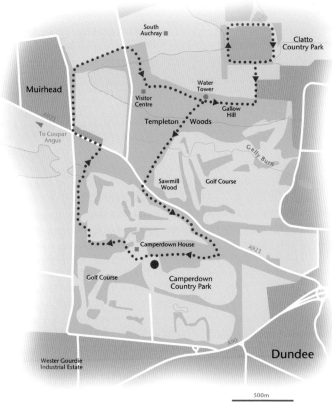

South Auchray ■

Clatto Country Park

Muirhead

Water Tower

Visitor Centre

Gallow Hill

Templeton ■ Woods

To Coupar Angus

Gelly Burn

Sawmill Wood

Golf Course

Camperdown House

A923

Golf Course

Camperdown Country Park

Wester Gourdie Industrial Estate

A90

Dundee

500m

footbridge beside a car park (Templeton Visitor Centre is straight ahead), turn left onto a broad track.

► This track follows blue waymarkers and soon passes the giant Gallow Hill Water Tower. From here, follow green waymarkers through the woodland to the outskirts of a small housing estate.

Bear left out of the wood and join a road that heads downhill towards Clatto Reservoir. Just before the reservoir, turn left into a car park and then right along a path that runs beside a watersports centre.

► Go down some steps to the left of the building and walk clockwise around the reservoir – home to an abundance of waterfowl. Once you've completed this waterside loop, retrace your steps to the watertower in Templeton Woods.

► Just past the tower, turn left (blue waymarker) to join a path that meanders downhill through pine woodland. Bear left at a fork and continue to the right of a golf course, soon crossing a bridge over the outflow of a pond. Turn right and then left onto a broad track, which passes through beech woodland on its way back to the A923.

► Cross the road with care and pass through a gate into Camperdown Country Park. Immediately, a junction is reached: turn left and follow the woodland path as it runs parallel with the A923 to the park's north entrance (and car park). Continue straight on, past another car park, to gain the main park road. Turn right here and return to Camperdown House.

Nautical Tales Covering an area of more than 400 acres – and containing nearly 200 species of trees – Camperdown Country Park is the largest public park in Dundee. Camperdown House itself was built between 1824 and 1828 and named after the Battle of Camperdown. It was at this battle that Dundee-born Admiral Adam Duncan and his Royal Navy fleet defeated the Dutch fleet in 1797 and saved the country from invasion. The name is derived from Kamperduin, a village on the coast of the Netherlands, close to the area of the naval engagement. Duncan's reward was a pension of £3000 a year – a handsome sum in those days – which his son, Robert Dundas, 2nd Viscount Duncan of Camperdown, used to build the neo-classical Camperdown House. The last occupant of the house was Georgiana Wilhelmina, Dowager Countess of Buckinghamshire, who died in 1937. The house contents were sold in a four-day auction in 1941 and the house and estate were purchased by Dundee Corporation in 1946.

The Sidlaws from Camperdown Country Park

Dundee Law

Desperate Dan

Dundee Law and Balgay Hill

Distance 7.75km/4.75 miles
Time 2 hours
Start/Finish Discovery Point,
Dundee GR NO404298
Terrain Pavement, woodland and
parkland paths and tracks
Map OS Landranger 54
Public transport Regular trains
and buses from across Scotland
to Dundee

As Scotland's fourth largest city,
Dundee has a wealth of beautiful
buildings, as well as a fascinating
recent history based around 'jute,
jam and journalism' – with
Desperate Dan, Dennis the Menace
and Oor Wullie among the
celebrated comic creations in local
publisher DC Thomson's stable.
This walk climbs through the city
to the vantage point of Dundee Law
and also visits Balgay Hill, home
to the UK's only full-time public
observatory.

► The walk begins beside the historic
Royal Research Ship Discovery, moored
by the banks of the Tay at Discovery
Point. With much of Britain's whaling
fleet built and based in Dundee at the
time, it was here in the late 1800s that
the Royal Geographical Society
commissioned the construction of a
vessel specifically designed to explore
Antarctica – at the time one of the last

unexplored corners of the world. At its
helm, when launched in 1901, was one
Robert Falcon Scott.

► Cross the A991 at Riverside
roundabout onto Dock Street. Turn left
onto Crichton Street and climb past the
Overgate Centre. Swing right onto High
Street beside the Caird Hall – named
after Sir James Caird who amassed his
fortune through the jute trade – and
then left onto Reform Street, passing a
statue of comic-book stalwart, Desperate
Dan. Continue along Reform Street to its
end beside the stunning McManus Art
Gallery and a statue of Robert Burns.

► Here, turn left onto Meadowside,
passing the DC Thomson building and
the Howff Cemetery where Greyfriar's
Monastery used to stand (after the
monastery was burnt down, Mary Queen
of Scots gifted the land to the city).

► Turn right onto Constitution Road,
walk past the University of Abertay and
through an underpass beneath the A991.
Head right, up a flight of steps, back
onto Constitution Road which then
climbs steeply onto Upper Constitution
Street, culminating at its junction with
Kinghorne Road.

► Turn right, then left onto Law Road.
Take the first left (still Law Road) to
climb past allotments, ignoring a path

127

Law of the Land Rising to a height of 174m, Dundee Law – part of an extinct volcano – is a familiar city landmark. With its key defensive position, the Law was the site of an Iron Age hill fort, while it was also well used by the Romans, possibly as a look-out post. In the 1820s, the Law had a 300m-long tunnel driven through its eastern side to accommodate the Dundee & Newtyle Railway, although this only operated until the 1860s when a new railway line was built to skirt the hill. Today, the summit is adorned by an impressive war memorial, with its beacon lit every year on 25 September (to remember the many local men who served in the 4th Battalion of the Black Watch and lost their lives in the Battle of Loos in 1915), 24 October (United Nations Day), Armistice Day and Remembrance Sunday.

on the right. At the next path, turn right and climb steeply up steps to Dundee Law, which provides panoramic views across the city and a good portion of the River Tay.

▶ Walk around the front of the war memorial and turn left to join a path that heads steeply down steps to cross a single-track road. A path then descends past West Law allotments onto Law Steps, which in turn takes you down across several side streets, to eventually reach Lochee Road.

▶ Turn left, then right onto Tullideph Road, continuing the short distance to City Road. Turn left here, then right to follow Pentland Avenue as far as Scott Street where a right turn leads into Balgay Park. The park was opened in 1871 by the Earl of Dalhousie as a means to help improve the health of the city's mill workers.

▶ Almost immediately, turn right onto a path signposted for the Mills Observatory. The path climbs steadily through woodland to a broader track. Take a left here, keep right at a fork, then left at the next fork. Continue to the observatory, which opened in 1935, having been funded by the estate of local linen manufacturer John Mills – a keen amateur astronomer who once had his own private observatory on Dundee Law.

▶ Retrace your steps to Scott Street and immediately bear right onto Balgay Road to head past Victoria Park. Turn left onto Blackness Road and walk along a line of attractive tenements. As Blackness Road swings right at Bellfield Street fork left and continue to Hawkhill. Head left, then left again onto Horsewater Wynd, before going right onto Guthrie Street (to the left on West Henderson Wynd is the Scottish Jute Museum).

▶ Follow Guthrie Street – once home to numerous flax mills – across Marketgait onto Ward Road and then Meadowside. Turn right onto Reform Street and retrace your steps to Discovery Point.

The Sidlaws from Auchterhouse Hill

Tay Estuary from Craigowl

Auchterhouse Hill, Balluderon Hill and Craigowl

Distance 7.5km/4.5 miles

Time 2 hours 30

Start/Finish Balkello Community Woodland Car Park GR NO365385

Terrain Woodland and hill paths and tracks

Map OS Landranger 54

Public transport None to start

Part of the Sidlaw range, Auchterhouse Hill and Craigowl are the high points of this great walk. Together with the lower Balluderon Hill, these summits create a formidable barrier to the north of Dundee and offer views across much of Tayside, wider Perthshire and the mountains that frame the Angus Glens. Good paths line the route.

► The walk starts from the car park at Balkello Community Woodland, a wonderfully biodiverse area of native tree around 2.4km east of Kirkton of Auchterhouse. Balkello translates from Gaelic as 'Place of the Monk's Cell', which hints at its past inhabitants.

► From the car park's far left corner, head through a gate and follow a broad, gravel path into the woodland. At a fork, bear left onto a path, which climbs gradually through the trees. Once through a gap in a wall, immediately turn right onto a grassy path, with Balluderon Hill ahead. Exit the woodland at a fork, bearing right to climb steadily to a junction. Turn left and continue along a path which ascends gently as it traverses the lower slopes of Balluderon Hill.

► At the next fork, head right where a good path continues to a saddle between Auchterhouse and Balluderon Hills, culminating at two gates. Take the gate on the left and follow a path through heather to the left of a fence. The path swings left away from the fence and climbs to a junction. Turn sharp right here and follow another path as it ascends gradually northwest, with the slopes of Auchterhouse Hill ahead. Go left at the next fork for a final fairly steep pull to the summit.

Prophetic Hills The Sidlaws run for roughly 50km from Kinnoull Hill, by Perth, to Forfar and are a popular stomping ground for Dundonians. Pronounced locally as 'The Seedlees', the range includes Dunsinane, a modest-sized hill (with a ruined hill fort on top) made famous by a line in Shakespeare's *Macbeth*: 'Macbeth shall never vanquish'd be until Great Birnam wood to high Dunsinane hill shall come against him'.

► Having enjoyed the views, retrace your steps to the saddle between Auchterhouse and Balluderon Hills. Pass through the gate, cross the outbound track and take the right branch of a fork to follow a steep, stony path to the 397m summit of Balluderon Hill – marked by a stone cairn and view indicator that commemorates local poet and author, Sydney Scroggie. There are uninterrupted views across Dundee and beyond from here.

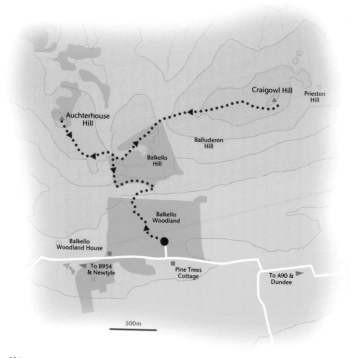

▶ Continue past the cairn and head straight on at a junction of paths to travel northeast across heather moorland, soon descending sharply. Go through a gate and bear left at a fork to climb steeply through the heather towards Craigowl, passing a single Scots pine.

▶ It's a long pull, but the incline eases in time. Cross a stile and follow the path a short distance to reach the rounded summit of Craigowl – at 455m, the highest point in the Sidlaws. Although marred by radio masts, the summit is a great vantage point, with the eye drawn, in particular, to the long finger of the Tay as it enters the North Sea at Tentsmuir Point.

▶ From the summit of Craigowl, retrace your steps over Balluderon Hill and down to the saddle used earlier in the walk to access the summit of Auchterhouse Hill. Turn left onto the outbound path and return through Balkello Woodland to the car park.

Syd of the Sidlaws Adorning the summit of Balluderon Hill is a cairn dedicated to the life of William Sydney Scroggie, or Syd as he was affectionately known. Born in BC, Canada in 1919, he moved to Dundee with his mother shortly after and went on to become a passionate walker and climber. After leaving school, he worked for the publisher DC Thomson and then served in Italy during World War II, where he was injured by a mine and lost a leg and the sight in both his eyes. Undeterred, Syd was soon back in the hills notching more than 600 ascents, including many in his beloved Sidlaws. He also became a poet and author, with published works including *The Cairngorms Scene and Unseen* (1989) and a collection of poetry, *Give Me the Hills* (1978). Syd unveiled the cairn built in his honour in 2000 when, aged 81, he climbed Balluderon Hill, guided by his second wife. Syd died in 2006.

Broughty Ferry from Barnhill

Broughty Ferry and Monifieth

Distance 10.75km/6.75 miles
Time 3 hours
Start/Finish Broughty Ferry Harbour
GR NO464305
Terrain Pavement, coastal paths,
cycle/walkway
Map OS Landranger 54
Public transport Regular Stagecoach
Service 73A from Dundee and
Arbroath to Broughty Ferry

**Overlooking the Tay as it empties
into the North Sea, the historic
towns of Broughty Ferry and
Monifieth are linked by a fine stretch
of coast. This easy walking route
journeys around attractive Monifieth
before returning along the northern
banks of the Firth of Tay to Broughty
Ferry Harbour, which is dominated
by a striking castle.**

► From the harbour, head along Castle
Approach (to the left of Broughty Castle)
to access The Esplanade. Turn left and
either walk northeast along the sand or

The Esplanade (be aware that dogs are
restricted from sections of the beach
during the seabird breeding season). If
following The Esplanade, continue past
Castle Terrace to reach a small car park on
the right. If walking along the beach
come off at the car park as it then
becomes quite stony.

► Keeping to the right edge of the car
park, head through parkland past Barnhill
Sands to a pavement. Turn right and then
bear right onto a cycle/walkway which
continues through more parkland with
Monifieth and the long stretch of Barry
Sands coming into view ahead. There are
also fine views across the firth to Tayport
and Tentsmuir Forest.

► The walkway swings left, then right to
run alongside a railway line, passing
under a bridge at Balmossie Station and
then crossing a bridge over the Dighty
Water. Continue until you come to
another bridge just before a caravan park
at Monifieth.

....

Ferry Tales Broughty Ferry grew as a small fishing port during the 17th and 18th
centuries, but expanded considerably as a holiday resort after the Dundee to Arbroath
Railway Line opened in 1838. Many of Dundee's jute merchants bought homes here,
considering 'the Ferry' to be a healthier place to live than the heavily industrialised city.
Broughty Ferry's small harbour is dominated by Broughty Castle, which dates back to
around 1495. Built by the Gray family, the castle has a typically colourful history that
includes occupation by invading English armies, ownership by two different railway
companies and its purchase and rearming by the War Office in 1851 to protect Dundee
from the French. It is now a museum operated by Dundee City Council.

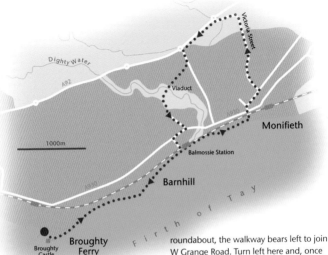

► Turn left and cross this bridge over the railway line to arrive at the junction of Maule Street and Ferry Road. Continue straight on to join Albert Street and then turn right onto Hill Street. Follow this quiet street through Monifieth before going left onto Victoria Street. Climb gradually past Ashludie Hospital and out of Monifieth, where lovely views open out across the Angus countryside.

► Victoria Street eventually swings left to reach a large roundabout fed by Arbroath Road (A92). Bear left onto a cycle/walkway, signposted 'Seven Arches Viaduct', and walk alongside the A92 for a few hundred metres. At the next roundabout, the walkway bears left to join W Grange Road. Turn left here and, once a short distance beyond Lawers Drive, turn right (through a barrier) to link up with another cycle/walkway. Follow this in between houses and then across the Seven Arches Viaduct (once part of the old Dundee to Forfar Railway Line), which passes high over the Dighty Water.

► The walkway then drops down to a crossroads. Turn left for Barnhill and follow a lane past Monifieth High School and its playing fields. Continue straight on along Panmurefield Road as far as Ferry Road (A930). Turn right, walk along Ferry Road, then turn left onto South Balmossie Street. At Balmossie Station, cross the bridge over the railway line, rejoin the outbound path and retrace your steps to Broughty Ferry Harbour.

Broughty Castle

Newburgh and the Tay

Newburgh

Distance **4.25km/2.75 miles**
Time **1 hour 15**
Start/Finish **Laing Library, High Street, Newburgh GR NO235184**
Terrain **Pavement, coastal and field-edge paths, single-track road**
Maps **OS Landranger 58 and 59**
Public transport **Regular Stagecoach Service 36 from Glenrothes and Perth to Newburgh**

This short, scenic walk explores the historic town of Newburgh, situated on the south bank of the Tay opposite Mugdrum Island. The route uses good paths, including sections of the Fife Coastal Path, and offers fine views over the Inner Firth, as well as excellent opportunities for spotting wildlife.

▶ Facing the Laing Library on the High Street (A913), turn left and walk through the town to climb to a car park. Look for a flight of steps that descends from the car park, and join a red gravel path that travels through open parkland. At a junction, turn left, then immediately right and descend to another junction. Turn right, exit the park through a gate and take the first left (signposted 'Fife Coastal Path') towards the River Tay. Turn right onto a paved path and walk along the shoreline as far as West Shore Road.

▶ Turn left, then right onto The Neuk and head past several small jetties along Beckett's Pier. Once across Albany Terrace and past Newburgh Football Ground, bear left onto a rougher path as it passes between the shore and football pitches, with lovely views of the surrounding countryside. As the Fife Coastal Path turns to the right, continue straight on along the Tay, the riverbanks

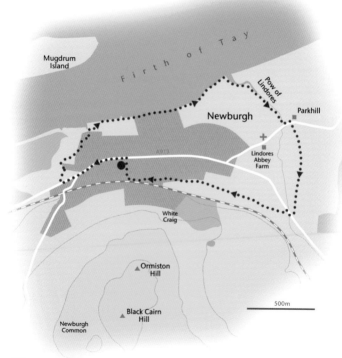

ined with reeds – an ideal habitat for a range of water birds.

► The narrow riverside path soon swings right and travels inland along the Pow of Lindores to reach Abbey Road at Parkmill (the nearby ruins of Lindores Abbey are well worth a visit).

► To continue the walk, turn left, head a few metres along the pavement and then turn right to rejoin the Fife Coastal Path as far as Cupar Road. Leaving the coastal path once again, turn right, head over a bridge and cross Cupar Road with care to join a lane that swings right past some houses before passing through a gate. From here, a rough track begins a steady climb. As the track swings left, continue straight on along a grassy path and go over a stile into a field.

► A public right of way crosses the field and passes beneath an old railway line to a stile beside a gate on the outskirts of Newburgh. Once across, a narrow path continues over a grassy embankment. Beyond a gap in a fence, go left, then immediately right and walk downhill to a lane. Turn left and follow this as it climbs gently, with superb views of Newburgh and the Tay, before bearing right onto a single-track road that comes in from the left. Continue to Hill Road, turn right and drop back down to the High Street.

....

Not So New Town Its name may suggest a relatively recent history, but this lovely Fife town actually dates back to around the 12th century when the 1st Earl of Huntingdon established the Tironensian Lindores Abbey as a daughter house of Kelso Abbey. Almost immediately the monks began making whisky – a commission from King James IV to the friar of Lindores Abbey in 1494 is the earliest record of whisky being distilled – and growing fruit. Today, many of the gardens in Newburgh have orchards that contain trees dating back to the original plantings, while a fruit market still runs from August to October each year. This market tradition began in 1266 when Alexander III granted the town burgh status and the right to hold weekly markets. Later, fishing became important to Newburgh's development, with the quayside home to around 40 fishing boats during the 19th century. Today, Newburgh is dominated by its attractive High Street, which is home to some fine buildings, including the Laing Library and Museum – gifted to the town by local historian and benefactor, Alexander Laing.

River Tay at Newburgh

Morton Lochs

Distance **7.25km/4.5 miles**
Time **1 hour 45**
Start/Finish **William Street, Tayport GR NO458288**
Terrain **Pavement, woodland and golf course paths and tracks**
Map **OS Landranger 54**
Public transport **Regular Stagecoach Service 96 from St Andrews and Dundee to Tayport**

A wonderfully tranquil wildlife haven at the western extremity of Tentsmuir National Nature Reserve, the reed-fringed Morton Lochs are popular with birdwatchers and walkers. This colourful walk is served by fine paths throughout.

► From Tayport town centre, walk along the B945 (which starts as William Street and becomes Queen Street) before turning left onto Maitland Street. At a roundabout, continue straight on to join Mill Lane which proceeds towards the shoreline. Once at the Promenade, head right to walk along the Tay Estuary, passing through a car park and into Tayport Links Caravan Park.

► Continue along the road (now Links Road North) all the way through the caravan site and then parkland to reach a junction with Shanwell Road South. Turn right here, walk past the entrance to a factory and then head left through a

gate onto a public path that runs through Scotscraig Golf Course. Follow this, bearing left at a fork beside some golf buildings to exit the course through another gate.

► Continue along a wide grassy track, past buildings at Garpit Farm. Beyond a gate, bear left and follow a wooded path through another gate into Tentsmuir National Nature Reserve. Continue straight on along the path through mixed woodland to reach a gate on the right. Head through the gate and walk a short distance to reach Morton Lochs and hides.

► Once you've checked out the hides, retrace your steps to the main track, turn right and walk through woodland to reach another hide and then a junction. Go left here and, once opposite a car park and an old railway arch, turn left where a lovely path heads north.

► The path soon bears left at a fork and returns to the outbound track. Turn right and retrace your steps out of the reserve, through the golf course and back to Shanwell Road. Turn left and continue along Shanwell Road as it swings left onto Nelson Street. At a roundabout, bear left to return to Maitland Street and then turn right onto Queen Street, following this back to William Street and Tayport town centre.

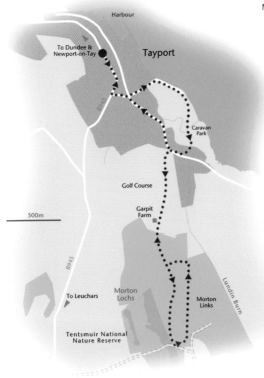

After the Flood Before Tentsmuir Forest was planted in the 1950s, the Morton Lochs site was part of an ancient area of dune heath. The three lochs themselves were created in 1906 by local landowners, the Christies, who flooded the area for fishing. The lochs quickly became a freshwater habitat for a variety of wildlife, in particular attracting large numbers of breeding and wintering wildfowl. Their importance was recognised in 1952 when Morton Lochs became a National Nature Reserve (only the second in Britain at the time). With four wildlife hides, there is ample opportunity to sit quietly and watch for otter, kingfisher, marsh harrier, goldeneye and many other species attracted by these food-rich waters.

Morton Lochs

Common Birdsfoot Trefoil

Harebell

Woodland at Morton Lochs

Selfheal

Abertay Sands

Tayport and Tentsmuir

Distance **11.25km/7 miles**
Time **3 hours**
Start/Finish **William Street, Tayport
GR NO458288**
Terrain **Pavement, woodland and
coastal paths and tracks**
Map **OS Landranger 54**
Public transport **Regular Stagecoach
Service 96 from Dundee and
St Andrews to Tayport**

A fascinating ever-changing
landscape of forest, dune and
beach, Tentsmuir National Nature
Reserve is a rewarding place to visit
at any time of year. It is also wildlife-
rich, with the grey and common
seals that loaf on sandbanks at low
tide one of the many natural
spectacles to be enjoyed.

▶ Starting from Tayport town centre
head along the B945 (which starts as
William Street and becomes Queen
Street) before turning left onto Maitland
Street. At a roundabout, continue
straight on to join Mill Lane which
proceeds towards the shoreline. Once at
the Promenade, head right and pass
through a car park and into Tayport
Links Caravan Park.

▶ Continue along the road (now Links
Road North) all the way through the

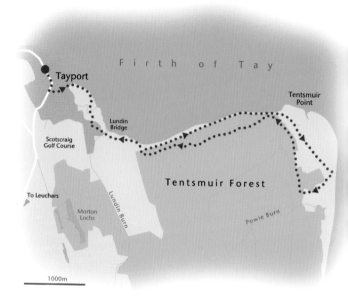

caravan site and then parkland to reach a junction with Shanwell Road South. Turn left here, cross Lundin Bridge and bear left at a fork around a barrier to follow a broad, stony track that runs parallel with the shoreline towards Tentsmuir National Nature Reserve.

▶ Keep an eye out for the many concrete anti-tank defences built here during World War II, although you might find yourself equally distracted by views across the Tay to Broughty Castle and the rolling Sidlaw Hills.

▶ Bear left at a fork, then right at another fork to gain a barrier at the edge of the reserve. Once around the barrier, follow the first path on the left as it runs east between woodland and sand dunes. In due course, the path swings sharply right. At this point leave the path and continue straight on along the beach for approximately 100m (if the tide is in, keep to the top of the beach) to join a sandy path that carries on alongside the woodland, eventually rounding Tentsmuir Point.

► The path then runs south, with wonderful views across Abertay Sands – a series of wispy sandbanks that can be seen stretching eastwards for some miles at low tide. Continue straight on at a gate, heading through the marram grass to a fork. Go right here and pass a wind pump (used to keep the rare dune slack habitat flooded for the benefit of specialist plants) to reach a wide grassy path.

► At a crossroads, continue straight on and walk just to the left of Tentsmuir Forest to a fork beside some concrete defences. Bear left and walk through the dunes to reach a delightful section of beach – an area where seals are often seen hauled out at low tide. Return to the fork and head left through the concrete defences.

► Head west along an indistinct path to the southern corner of a pocket of woodland, where a narrow, grassy path runs towards Tentsmuir Forest. At a fork go right, the path now less distinct. However, a broader track is soon picked up to reach a gate (known as 'Dave's Gate'). Go through this to a junction, turn right and follow the track through picturesque woodland, continuing straight on at Junction 5.

► Walk past the March Stone – a 200-year-old standing stone erected to mark a boundary for fishing rights – and continue as the track rounds Tentsmuir Point, veering left to Junction 4. Take the left fork (signposted 'Lundin Bridge') to join a broad forest track that meanders west for around 2.5km through wildlife-rich woodland, eventually returning to the barrier at the entrance to the reserve. From here, retrace your steps over Lundin Bridge and back to Tayport.

Pilgrim's Port The town of Tayport, sitting at the mouth of the River Tay, has only been known as such since the mid-19th century. Previous incarnations include Scotscraig, South Ferry and Ferry-Port on Craig – all referencing the ferry service which used to run across the Tay to Broughty Ferry, or the crag on which the town is built. It is thought that a ferry service was already in place when pilgrims journeyed between St Andrews and the newly formed Arbroath Abbey in the 12th century. An almost continuous ferry service was maintained in one form or another – at one point it was part of a railway ferry service for passengers travelling between Edinburgh and Aberdeen – up until 1920.

157

Broughty Ferry from Tayport

Index